Raspberry Pi IoT Projects

Prototyping Experiments for Makers

John C. Shovic, PhD

Apress®

Raspberry Pi IoT Projects: Prototyping Experiments for Makers

John C. Shovic
Liberty Lake, Washington, USA

ISBN-13 (pbk): 978-1-4842-1378-0
DOI 10.1007/978-1-4842-1377-3

ISBN-13 (electronic): 978-1-4842-1377-3

Library of Congress Control Number: 2016949468

Distributed to the book trade worldwide by Springer Science+Business Media New York, 233 Spring Street, 6th Floor, New York, NY 10013. Phone 1-800-SPRINGER, fax (201) 348-4505, e-mail orders-ny@springer-sbm.com, or visit www.springer.com. Apress Media, LLC is a California LLC and the sole member (owner) is Springer Science + Business Media Finance Inc (SSBM Finance Inc). SSBM Finance Inc is a **Delaware** corporation.

For information on translations, please e-mail rights@apress.com, or visit www.apress.com.

Apress and friends of ED books may be purchased in bulk for academic, corporate, or promotional use. eBook versions and licenses are also available for most titles. For more information, reference our Special Bulk Sales–eBook Licensing web page at www.apress.com/bulk-sales.

Any source code or other supplementary materials referenced by the author in this text is available to readers at www.apress.com. For detailed information about how to locate your book's source code, go to www.apress.com/source-code/.

To my best friend Laurie and also to my cat Panther,
who is an IOT device by himself.

Contents at a Glance

Contents

About the Author

Dr. John C. Shovic is currently Chief Technical Officer of SwitchDoc Labs, a company specializing in technical products for the Maker Movement and the IOT; and InstiComm, a company specializing in mobile medical software solutions for health practitioners. He was also Chief Technology Strategist at Stratus Global Partners with a focus on supplying expertise in computer security regulatory and technical areas to health care providers. He has worked in the industry for over thirty years and has founded seven companies: Advanced Hardware Architectures, TriGeo Network Security, Blue Water Technologies, MiloCreek, InstiComm, SwitchDoc Labs, and bankCDA. As a founding member of the bankCDA board of directors, he currently serves as the chairman of the technology committee. He has also served as a Professor of Computer Science at Eastern Washington University, Washington State University, and the University of Idaho. Dr. Shovic has given over eighty invited talks and has published over seventy papers on a variety of topics on Arduinos/Raspberry Pi's, HIPAA, GLB, computer security, computer forensics, and embedded systems.

About the Technical Reviewer

Gheorghe Chesler is a Senior Software Engineer with expertise in Quality Assurance, System Automation, Performance Engineering, and e-Publishing. He works at ServiceNow as a Senior Performance Engineer, and is a principal technical consultant for Plural Publishing, a medical-field publishing company. His preferred programming language is Perl (so much so that he identifies with the Perl mascot, hence the camel picture), but also worked on many Java and Objective-C projects.

Acknowledgments

The author would like to acknowledge the hard work of the APress editorial team in putting this book together. He would also like to acknowledge the hard work of the Raspberry Pi Foundation and the Arduino group for putting together products and communities that help to make the Internet Of Things more accessible to the general public. Hurray for the democratization of technology!

Introduction

The Internet Of Things (IOT) is a complex concept made up of many computers and many communication paths. Some IOT devices are connected to the Internet and some are not. Some IOT devices form swarms that communicate among themselves. Some are designed for a single purpose, while some are more general purpose computers. This book is designed to show you the IOT from the inside out. By building IOT devices, the reader will understand the basic concepts and will be able to innovate using the basics to create his or her own IOT applications.

These included projects will show the reader how to build their own IOT projects and to expand upon the examples shown. The importance of Computer Security in IOT devices is also discussed and various techniques for keeping the IOT safe from unauthorized users or hackers. The most important takeaway from this book is in building the projects yourself.

Chapters at a Glance

In this book, we built examples of all the major parts of simple and complex IOT devices.

In Chapter 1, the basic concepts of IOT are explained in basic terms, and you will learn what parts and tools are needed to start prototyping your own IOT devices.

In Chapter 2, you'll learn how to sense the environment with electronics and that even the behavior of simple LightSwarm type of devices can be very unpredictable.

Chapter 3 introduces important concepts about how to build real systems that can respond to power issues and programming errors by the use of good system design and watchdogs.

Chapter 4 turns a Raspberry Pi into a battery-powered device that senses iBeacons and controls the lighting in a house while reporting your location to a server.

In Chapter 5, you'll do IOT the way the big boys do by connecting up to the IBM BlueMix IOT Server and sending our biometric pulse rates up for storage and display.

In Chapter 6, we'll build a small RFID Inventory system and use standard protocols like MQTT to send information to a Raspberry Pi, a complete IOT product.

Chapter 7 shows the dark side of the IOT, Computer Security. The way you protect your IOT device from hackers and network problems is the most difficult part of IOT device and system design.

Are you totally secure? You will never know. Plan for it.

The reference appendix provides resources for further study and suggestions for other projects.

CHAPTER 1

▨ ▨ ▨

Introduction to IOT

Chapter Goal: Understand What the IOT Is and How to Prototype IOT Devices

Topics Covered in This Chapter:

- What is IOT

- Choosing a Raspberry Pi Model

- Choosing your IOT Device

- Characterization of IOT Devices

- Buying the right tools to deal with Hardware

- Writing code in Python and in the Arduino IDE

The IOT is a name for the vast collection of "things" that are being networked together in the home and workplace (up to 20 billion by 2020 according to Gardner, a technology consulting firm). That is a very vast collection. And they may be underestimating it.

We all have large numbers of computers in a modern house. I just did a walkthrough of my house, ignoring my office (which is filled with another ~100 computers). I found 65 different devices having embedded computers. I'm sure I missed some of them. Now of those computer-based devices, I counted 20 of them that have IP addresses, although I know that I am missing a few (such as the thermostat). So in a real sense, this house has 20 IOT devices. And it is only 2016 as of the writing of this book. With over 100 million households in the United States alone, 20 billion IOT devices somehow don't seem so many.

So what are the three defining characteristics of the IOT?

- Networking - these IOT devices talk to one another (M2M communication) or to servers located in the local network or on the Internet. Being on the network allows the device the common ability to consume and produce data.

- Sensing - IOT devices sense something about their environment.

Electronic supplementary material The online version of this chapter (doi:10.1007/978-1-4842-1377-3_1) contains supplementary material, which is available to authorized users.

J. C. Shovic, *Raspberry Pi IoT Projects*, DOI 10.1007/978-1-4842-1377-3_1

1

- Actuators - IOT devices that do something. Lock doors, beep, turn lights on, or turn the TV on.

Of course, not every IOT device will have all three, but these are the characteristics of what we will find out there.

Is the IOT valuable? Will it make a difference? Nobody is sure what the killer application will be, but people are betting huge sums of money that there will be a killer application. Reading this book and doing the projects will teach you a lot about the technology and enable you to build your own IOT applications.

Choosing a Raspberry Pi Model

The Raspberry Pi family of single board computers (see Figure 1-1) is a product of the Raspberry Pi Foundation (RaspberryPi.org). They have sold over 9 million of these small, inexpensive computers. The Raspberry Pi runs a number of different operating systems, the most common of which is the Raspian release of Unbuntu Linux.

Figure 1-1. *Raspberry Pi 2*

Like Windows, Linux is a multitasking operating system, but unlike Windows, it is an open source system. You can get all the source code and compile it if you wish, but I would not recommend that to a beginner.

One of the best parts of the Raspberry Pi is that there are a huge number of device and sensor drivers available, which makes it a good choice for building IOT projects, especially using it as a server for your IOT project. The Raspberry Pi is not a low-power device, which limits its usage as an IOT device. However, it is still a great prototyping device and a great server.

There is a rather bewildering variety of Raspberry Pi boards available. I suggest for this book that you get a Raspberry PI 2 or Raspberry Pi 3. While the $5.00 Raspberry Pi Zero is tempting, it takes quite a bit of other hardware to get it to the point where it is usable. While the Raspberry Pi 3 is more expensive ($35), it comes with a WiFi interface built in and extra USB ports.

Note that we are using the Raspberry Pi A+ for building the IOTWeatherPi weather station later in this book. The reason for that is power consumption: one-half to one-third of the power used by the more powerful Raspberry Pi models.

There are many great tutorials on the Web for setting up your Raspberry Pi and getting the operating system software running.

Choosing an IOT Device

If you think the list of Raspberry Pi boards available is bewildering, then wait until you look at the number of IOT devices that are available. While each offering is interesting and has unique features, I am suggesting the following devices for your first projects in the IOT. Note that I selected these based upon the ability to customize the software and to add your own devices without hiding ALL the complexity, hence reducing the learning involved. That is why I am not using Lego-type devices in this book.

We will be using the following:

- ESP8266-based boards (specifically the Adafruit Huzzah ESP8266)

- Arduino Uno and Arduino Mega2560 boards

Characterizing an IOT Project

When looking at a new project, the first thing to do to understand an IOT project is to look at the six different aspects for characterizing an IOT project.

- Communications

- Processor Power

- Local Storage

- Power Consumption

- Functionality

- Cost

When I think about these characteristics, I like to rate each one on a scale from 1–10, 1 being the least suitable for IOT and 10 being the most suitable for IOT applications. Scoring each one forces me to think carefully about how a given project falls on the spectrum of suitability.

Communications

Communications are important to IOT projects. In fact, communications are core to the whole genre. There is a trade-off for IOT devices. The more complex the protocols and higher the data rates, the more powerful processor you need and the more electrical power the IOT device will consume.

TCP/IP base communications (think web servers; HTTP-based commutation (like REST servers); streams of data; UDP - see Chapter 2) provide the most flexibility and functionality at a cost of processor and electrical power.

Low-power BlueTooth and Zigbee types of connections allow much lower power for connections with the corresponding decrease in bandwidth and functionality.

IOT projects can be all over the map with requirements for communication flexibility and data bandwidth requirements.

IOT devices having full TCP/IP support are rated the highest in this category, but will probably be marked down in other categories (such as Power Consumption).

Processor Power

There are a number of different ways of gauging processor power. Processor speed, processor instruction size, and operating system all play in this calculation. For most IOT sensor and device applications, you will not be limited by processor speed as they are all pretty fast. However, there is one exception to this. If you are using encryption and decryption techniques (see Chapter 7), then those operations are computationally expensive and require more processor power to run. The trade-off can be that you have to transmit or receive data much more slowly because of the computational requirements of encrypting/decrypting the data. However, for many IOT projects, this is just fine.

Higher processor power gives you the highest ratings in this category.

Local Storage

Local storage refers to all three of the main types of storage: RAM, EEPROM, and Flash Memory.

RAM (Random Access Memory) is high-data rate, read/writable memory, generally used for data and stack storage during execution of the IOT program. EEPROM (Electrically Erasable Programmable Read Only Memory) is used for writing small amounts of configuration information for the IOT device to be read on power up. Flash Memory is generally used for the program code itself. Flash is randomly readable (as the code executes, for example), but can only be written in large blocks and very slowly. Flash is what you are putting your code into with the Arduino IDE (see Chapter 2).

The amount of local storage (especially RAM) will add cost to your IOT Device. For prototyping, the more the merrier. For deployment, less is better as it will reduce your cost.

Power Consumption

Power consumption is the bane of all IOT devices. If you are not plugging your IOT device in the wall, then you are running off of batteries or solar cells and every single milliwatt counts in your design. Reducing power consumption is a complex topic that is well beyond the introductory projects in this book. However, the concepts are well understood by the following:

- Put your processor in sleep mode as much as possible.

- Minimize communication outside of your device.

- Try to be interrupt driven and not polling driven.

- Scour your design looking for every unnecessary amount of current.

The higher the number in this category, the less power the IOT unit uses.

Functionality

This is kind of a catch-all category that is quite subjective. For example, having additional GPIOs (General Purpose Input Outputs) available is great for flexibility. I am continuously running into GPIO limitations with the Adafruit Huzzah ESP8266 as there are so few pins available. Having additional serial interfaces are very useful for debugging. Special hardware support for encryption and decryption can make device computer security much simpler. One of the things that I miss in most IOT prototyping system is software debugging support hardware.

I also include the availability of software libraries for a platform into this category. A ten means very high functionality; low numbers mean limited functionality.

Cost

What is an acceptable cost for your IOT device? That depends on the value of the device and the market for your device. A $2.50 price can be great for prototypes, but will be the death of the product in production. You need to size the price to the product and the market. High numbers are low-cost units and low numbers are higher-cost devices.

The Right Tools to Deal with Hardware

Anything is more difficult without the right tools. When you make the jump from just doing software to doing a software / hardware mix, here is a list of tools you should have:

- 30W adjustable temperature soldering iron - heating and connecting wires

- Soldering stand - to hold the hot soldering iron

- Solder, rosin-core, 0.031" diameter, 1/4 lb (100g) spool - to solder with

- Solder sucker -Useful in cleaning up mistakes

- Solder wick/braid 5 ft spool - Used along with the solder sucker to clean up soldering messes

- Panavise Jr - General purpose 360 degree mini-vise

- Digital Multimeter – Good all-around basic multimeter

- Diagonal cutters - Trimming of wires and leads

- Wire strippers - Tool for taking insulation off wires

- Micro needle-nose pliers - for bending and forming components

- Solid-core wire, 22AWG, 25 ft spools - black, red, and yellow for bread-boarding and wiring

Adafruit has an excellent beginners kit for $100 [https://www.adafruit.com/products/136]. Figure 1-2 shows the tools that are in it.

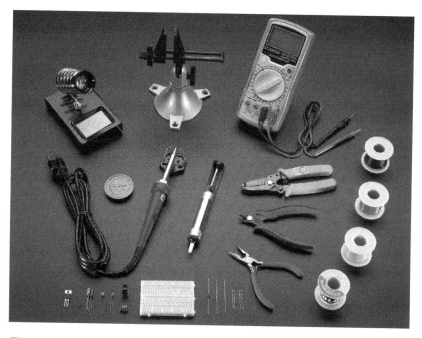

Figure 1-2. *Adafruit Electronics Toolkit*

Writing Code in Python and the Arduino IDE

All the code in this book is in two languages. Specifically, Python is used for the Raspberry Pi and C/C++ (don't be scared, there are many examples and resources) for the Arduino IDE.

Python is a high-level, general purpose programming language. It is designed to emphasize code readability, and it especially keeps you out of having loose pointers (a curse of all C/C++ programmers) and does the memory management for you. This is the programming language of choice for the Raspberry Pi. Python has the largest set of libraries for IOT and embedded system devices of any language for the Raspberry Pi. All of the examples in this book that use the Raspberry Pi, use Python. I am using Python 2.7 in this book, but it is relatively easy to convert to Python 3.5. However, it is not so trivial to find all the libraries for Python 3.5, so I suggest staying with Python 2.7.

Why are we using C++ for the majority of the IOT devices? There are four reasons for this:

- C programs are compiled into native code for these small devices, giving you much better control over size and timing. Python requires an interpreter, which is a large amount of code that would not fit on small IOT devices, such as the Arduino. On a Raspberry Pi, you may have a Gigabyte (GB) of RAM and 8GB of SD Card storage. On an IOT device, you might only 2,000 bytes (2K) and 32KB of code storage. That is a ratio of 500,000 to 1. That is why you need efficient code on IOT devices. Yes, there is MicroPython, but it is very limited and still uses more memory than most Arduino boards.

- When you program in C/C++, you are closer to the hardware and have better control of the timing of operations. This can be very important in some situations. One of the issues of Python is that of the memory garbage collector. Sometimes, your program will run out of memory and Python will invoke the garbage collector to clean up memory and set it up for reuse. This can cause your program to not execute in the time you expected. An interesting note is that the ESP8266 used in several chapters of this book also has a memory garbage collector, which can cause some issues in critical timing sequences. None of are known to exist in the code used in this book. Keeping fingers crossed, however.

- Libraries, libraries, libraries. You can find Arduino C/C++ libraries for almost any device and application you can imagine for IOT applications. The Arduino library itself is filled with large amounts of functionality, making it much easier to get your IOT application up and running.

7

- Finally, the Arduino IDE (Integrated Development Environment) is a good (but not great) environment for writing code for small devices. It has its quirks and some disadvantages. The number one disadvantage of the Arduino IDE is that it does not have a built-in debugger. Even with this significant disadvantage, it runs on Linux, Windows, and Mac, and we will use it in this book. The Arduino IDE is widely available, and there are many resources for learning and libraries designed for this. Other alternatives include Visual Micro (runs on Windows, built on Microsoft Visual Studio) and Eclipse (runs on Linux, Windows, and Mac). Eclipse can be a nightmare to set up and update, but they have made improvements in the past few years.

In This Book

What will we be doing in future chapters? We will be building real IOT projects that actually have a lot of functionality. Yes, it is fun to blink an LED, but it is only the first step to really doing interesting and useful things with all this new technology. Build an IOT weather station. Build an IOT light swarm. Build your own IOT device with your own sensors. It is all accessible and inexpensive and within your ability whether you are an engineer or not.

CHAPTER 2

▓ ▓ ▓

Sensing Your IOT Environment

Chapter Goal: Build Your First IOT Device
Topics Covered in This Chapter:

- Building an inexpensive IOT Sensor device based on the ESP8266 and Arduino IDE

- Setting up a simple Self-Organizing IOT Sensor Net

- Reading I2C sensor (light and color) on the Arduino devices

- Reading data from remote IOT sensors on the Raspberry Pi

- Using the Raspberry Pi for Monitoring and Debugging

- Displaying your Data on the screen and on an iPad

In this chapter, we build our first IOT device. This simple design, a light-sensor swarm, is easy to build and illustrates a number of IOT principles including the following:

- Distributed Control

- Self-Organization

- Passing Information to the Internet

- Swarm Behavior

The LightSwarm architecture is a simple and flexible scheme for understanding the idea of an IOT project using many simple small computers and sensors with shared responsibility for control and reporting. Note that in this swarm, communication with the Internet is handled by a Raspberry Pi. The swarm devices talk to each other, but not with the Internet. The Raspberry Pi is located on the same WiFi access point as the swarm, but could be located far away with some clever forwarding of packets through your WiFi router. In this case, since we have no computer security at all in this design (see Chapter 7 for information on making your IOT swarm and device more secure) and so we are sticking with the local network. The exception to this is the RasPiConnect LightSwarm control panel that can be located anywhere on the Internet and is secured by password control and could easily be sent via https, encrypting the individual XML packets.

© John C. Shovic 2016
J. C. Shovic, *Raspberry Pi IoT Projects*, DOI 10.1007/978-1-4842-1377-3_2

IOT Sensor Nets

One of the major uses of the IOT will be building nets and groups of sensors. Inexpensive sensing is just as big of a driver for the IOT as the development of inexpensive computers. The ability for a computer to sense its environment is the key to gathering information for analysis, action, or transmittal to the Internet. Sensor nets have been around in academia for many years, but now the dropping prices and availability of development tools are quickly moving sensor nets out to the mainstream. Whole industrial and academic conferences are now held on sensor nets [www.sensornets.org]. The market is exploding for these devices, and opportunities are huge for the creative person or group that can figure out how to make the sensor net that will truly drive consumer sales.

IOT Characterization of This Project

As I discussed in Chapter 1, the first thing to do to understand an IOT project is to look at our six different aspects of IOT. LightSwarm is a pretty simple project and can be broken down into the six components listed in Table 2-1.

Table 2-1. *LightSwarm Characterization (CPLPFC)*

Aspect	Rating	Comments
Communications	9	WiFi connection to Internet - can do ad-hoc mesh-type communication
Processor Power	7	80MHz XTensa Harvard Architecture CPU, ~80KB Data RAM / ~35KB of Instruction RAM / 200K ROM
Local Storage	6	4MB Flash (or 3MB file system!)
Power Consumption	7	~200mA transmitting, ~60mA receiving, no WiFi ~15mA, Standby ~1mA
Functionality	7	Partial Arduino Support (limited GPIO/Analog Inputs)
Cost	9	< $10 and getting cheaper

Ratings are from 1–10, 1 being the least suitable for IOT and 10 being the most suitable for IOT applications.

This gives us a CPLPFC rating of 7.2. This is calculated by averaging all six values together with equal weighting. This way is great for learning and experimenting, and could be deployed for some applications.

The ESP8266 is an impressive device having a built-in WiFi connection, a powerful CPU, and quite a bit of RAM and access to the Arduino libraries. It is inexpensive and will get cheaper as time goes on. It is a powerful device for prototyping IOT applications requiring medium levels of functionality.

How Does This Device Hook Up to the IOT?

The ESP8266 provides a WiFi transmitter/receiver, a TCP/IP stack, and firmware to support direction connections to a local WiFi access point that then can connect to the Internet. In this project, the ESP8266 will only be talking to devices on the local wireless network. -This is an amazing amount of functionality for less than $10 retail. These chips can be found for as little as $1 on the open market, if you want to roll your own printed circuit board.

What Is an ESP8266?

The ESP8266 is made by a company in China called Espressif [espressif.com]. They are a fabless semiconductor company that just came out of nowhere with the first generation of this chip and shook up the whole industry. Now all the major players are working on inexpensive versions of an IOT chip with WiFi connectivity.

The ESP8266 chip was originally designed for connected light bulbs but soon got used in a variety of applications, and ESP8266 modules are currently now the most popular solutions to add WiFi to IOT projects. While the ESP8266 has huge functionality and a good price, the amount of current consumed by the chip makes battery-powered solutions problematic.

The ESP8266 is enabling a whole new set of applications and communities with their innovative and inexpensive design (Figure 2-1).

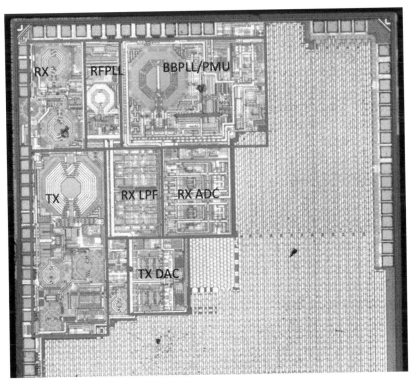

Figure 2-1. The ESP8266 die. (Courtesy of Hackaday.io)

11

We will be using a version of the ESP8266 on a breakout board designed by Adafruit (Figure 2-2). The board provides some connections, a built-in antenna, and some power regulation, all for less than $10.

Figure 2-2. *The Adafruit Huzzah ESP8266. (Courtesy of* adafruit.com*)*

The LightSwarm Design

There are two major design aspects of the LightSwarm project. First of all, each element of the swarm is based on an ESP8266 with a light sensor attached. The software is what makes this small IOT device into a swarm. In the following block diagram you can see the major two devices. I am using the Adafruit Huzzah breakout board for the ESP8266 [www.adafruit.com/product/2471]. Why use a breakout board? With a breakout board you can quickly prototype devices and then move to a less-expensive design in the future. The other electronic component (Figure 2-3) is a TCS34725 RGB light-sensor breakout board, also from Adafruit [www.adafruit.com/products/1334].

Figure 2-3. *TCS34725 Breakout Board. (Courtesy of adafruit.com)*

The addition of a sensor to a computer is what makes this project an IOT device. I am sensing the environment and then doing something with the information (determining which of the Swarm has the brightest light). Figure 2-4 shows the block diagram of a single Swarm element.

13

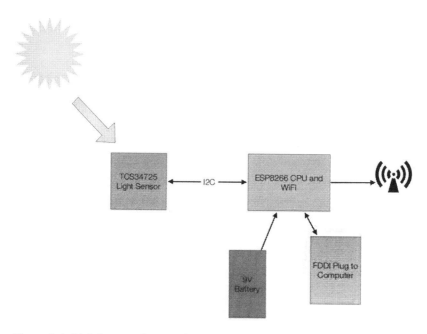

Figure 2-4. *LightSwarm Element Block Diagram*

Each of the LightSwarm devices in the swarm is identical. There are no software differences and no hardware differences. As you will see when we discuss the software, they vote with each other and compare notes and then elect the device that has the brightest light as the "Master," and then the "Master" turns the red LED on the device to show us who has been elected "Master." The swarm is designed so devices can drop out of the swarm, be added to the swarm dynamically, and the swarm adjusts to the new configuration. The swarm behavior (who is the master, how long it takes information about changing lights to propagate through the swarm, etc.) is rather complex. More complex than expected from the simple swarm device code. There is a lesson here: simple machines in groups can lead to large complex systems with higher-level behaviors based on the simple machines and the way they interact.

The behavior of the LightSwarm surprised me a number of times and it was sometimes very difficult to figure out what was happening, even with the Raspberry Pi logger. Figure 2-5 shows the complete LightSwarm including the Raspberry Pi.

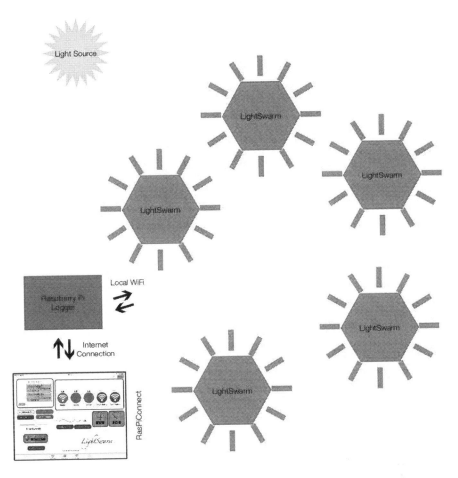

Figure 2-5. *The Light Swarm*

The Raspberry Pi in this diagram is not controlling the swarm. The Raspberry Pi gathers data from the swarm (the current "Master" device sends information to the Raspberry Pi), and then the Raspberry Pi can store the data and communicate it through the Internet, in this case to an iPad-based app called RasPiConnect [www.milocreek.com], which displays the current and historical state of the LightSwarm.

The LightSwarm project has an amazing amount of functionality and quirky self-organizing behavior for such a simple design.

Building Your First IOT Swarm

Table 2-2 lists the parts needed to build an IOT Swarm.

Table 2-2. *Swam Parts List*

Part Number	Count	Description	Approximate Cost per Board	Source
ESP8266 Huzzah Board	5	CPU / WiFi board	$10	www.adafruit.com/ products/2471
TCS34725 Breakout Board	5	I2C Light Sensor	$8	www.adafruit.com/ products/1334
FTDI Cable	1	Cable for programming the ESP8266 from PC/Mac	$18	www.adafruit.com/ products/70

Installing Arduino Support on the PC or Mac

The key to making this project work is the software. While there are many ways of programming the ESP8266 (MicroPython) [micropython.org], NodeMCU Lua interpreter [nodemcu.com/index_en.html], and the Arduino IDE (Integrated Development Environment) [www.arduino.cc/en/Main/Software]), I chose the Arduino IDE for its flexibility and the large number of sensor and device libraries available.

To install the Arduino IDE you need to do the following:

a. Download the Arduino IDE package for your computer and install the software [www.arduino.cc/en/Guide/HomePage].

b. Download the ESP libraries so you can use the Arduino IDE with the ESP breakout board. Adafruit has an excellent tutorial for installing the ESP8266 support for the Arduino IDE [learn.adafruit.com/adafruit-huzzah-esp8266-breakout/ using-arduino-ide].

Your First Sketch for the ESP8266

A great way of testing your setup is to run a small sketch that will blink the red LED on the ESP8266 breakout board. The red LED is hooked up to GPIO 0 (General Purpose Input Output pin 0) on the Adafruit board.

Open a new sketch using the Arduino IDE and place the following code into the code window, replacing the stubs provided when opening a new sketch. The code given here will make the red LED blink.

```
void setup() {
  pinMode(0, OUTPUT);
}

void loop() {
  digitalWrite(0, HIGH);
  delay(500);
  digitalWrite(0, LOW);
  delay(500);
}
```

If your LED is happily blinking away now, you have correctly followed all the tutorials and have the ESP8266 and the Arduino IDE running on your computer.

Next I will describe the major hardware systems and then dive into the software.

The Hardware

The main pieces of hardware in the swarm device are the following:

- ESP8266 - CPU/WiFi Interface

- TCS34725 - Light sensor

- 9V Battery - Power

- FTDI Cable - Programming and power

The ESP8266 communicates with other swarm devices by using the WiFi interface. The ESP8266 uses the I2C interface to communicate with the light sensor. The WiFi is a standard that is very common (although we use protocols to communicate that are NOT common). See the description of UDP (User Datagram Protocol) later in this chapter. The I2C bus interface is much less familiar and needs some explanation.

Reviewing the I2C Bus

An I2C bus is often used to communicate with chips or sensors that are on the same board or located physically close to the CPU. It stands for standard Inter-IC device bus. The I2C was first developed by Phillips (now NXP Semiconductors). To get around licensing issues, often the bus will be called TWI (Two Wire Interface). SMBus, developed by Intel, is a subset of I2C that defines the protocols more strictly. Modern I2C systems take policies and rules from SMBus sometimes supporting both with minimal reconfiguration needed. The Raspberry Pi and the Arduino are both these kinds of devices. Even the ESP8266 used in this project can support both.

An I2C provides good support for slow, close peripheral devices that only need be addressed occasionally. For example, a temperature measuring device will generally only change very slowly and so is a good candidate for the use of I2C, where a camera will generate lots of data quickly and potentially changes often.

An I2C bus uses only two bidirectional open-drain lines (open-drain means the device can pull a level down to ground, but cannot pull the line up to Vdd. Hence the name open-drain). Thus a requirement of an I2C bus is that both lines are pulled up to Vdd. This is an important area and not properly pulling up the lines is the first and most common mistake you make when you first use an I2C bus. More on pullup resistors later in the next section. The two lines are SDA (Serial Data Line) and the SCL (Serial Clock Line). There are two types of devices you can connect to an I2C bus. They are Master devices and Slave devices. Typically, you have one Master device (the Raspberry Pi in our case) and multiple Slave devices, each with their individual 7-bit address (like 0x68 in the case of the DS1307). There are ways to have 10-bit addresses and multiple Master devices, but that is beyond the scope of this column. Figure 2-6 shows an I2C bus with devices and the master connected.

■ **SwitchDoc Note**   Vcc and Vdd mean the same. Gnd and Vss generally also both mean ground. There are historical differences, but today Vcc usually is one power supply, and if there is a second, they will call it Vdd.

When used on the Raspberry Pi, the Raspberry Pi acts as the Master and all other devices are connected as Slaves.

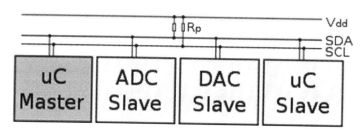

Figure 2-6. *An I2C bus with one Master (the ESP8266 in this case) and three Slave devices. Rps are the Pullup Resistors*

■ **SwitchDoc Note**   If you connect an Arduino to a Raspberry Pi, you need to be careful about voltage levels because the Raspberry Pi is a 3.3V device and the Arduino is a 5.0V device. The ESP8266 is a 3.3V device so you also need to be careful connecting an Arduino to an ESP8266. Before you do this, read this excellent tutorial [blog.retep. org/2014/02/15/connecting-an-arduino-to-a-raspberry-pi-using-i2c/].

The I2C protocol uses three types of messages:

- *Single message* where a master writes data to a slave;

- *Single message* where a master reads data from a slave;

- *Combined messages*, where a master issues at least two reads and/ or writes to one or more slaves.

Lucky for us, most of the complexity of dealing with the I2C bus is hidden by drivers and libraries.

Pullups on the I2C Bus

One important thing to consider on your I2C bus is a pullup resistor. The Raspberry Pi has 1.8K ohm (1k8) resistors already attached to the SDA and SCL lines, so you really shouldn't need any additional pullup resistors. However, you do need to look at your I2C boards to find out if they have pullup resistors. If you have too many devices on the I2C bus with their own pullups, your bus will stop working. The rule of thumb from Phillips is not to let the total pullup resistors in parallel be less than 1K (1k0) ohms. You can get a pretty good idea of what the total pullup resistance is by turning the power off on all devices and using an ohm meter to measure the resistance on the SCL line from the SCL line to Vdd.

Sensor Being Used

We are using the TCS34725, which has RGB and Clear light-sensing elements. Figure 2-7 shows the TCS34725 die with the optical sensor showing in the center of the figure. An IR blocking filter, integrated on-chip and localized to the color-sensing photodiodes, minimizes the IR spectral component of the incoming light and allows color measurements to be made accurately. The IR filter means you'll get much truer color than most sensors, since humans don't see IR. The sensor does see IR and thus the IR filter is provided. The sensor also has a 3,800,000:1 dynamic range with adjustable integration time and gain so it is suited for use behind darkened glass or directly in the light.

Figure 2-7. *The TCS34725 Chip Die*

This is an excellent inexpensive sensor ($8 retail from Adafruit on a breakout board) and forms the basis of our IOT sensor array. Of course, you could add many more sensors, but having one sensor that is easy to manipulate is perfect for our first IOT project. In Chapter 3, we add many more sensors to the Raspberry Pi computer for a complete IOT WeatherStation design.

3D Printed Case

One of the big changes in the way people build prototypes is the availability of inexpensive 3D printers. It used to be difficult to build prototype cases and stands for various electronic projects. Now it is easy to design a case in one of many types of 3D software and then print it out using your 3D printer. For the swarm, I wanted a partial case to hold the 9V battery, the ESP8266, and the light sensor. I used OpenSCAD [www.openscad.org] to do the design. OpenSCAD is a free 3D CAD system that appeals to programmers. Rather than doing the entire design in a graphical environment, you write code (consisting of various objects, joined together or subtracted from each other) that you then compile in the environment to form a design in 3D space. OpenSCAD comes with an IDE (Integrated Development Environment) and you place the code showing in Listing 2-1 in the editor, compile the code, and then see the results in the attached IDE as shown in Figure 2-8.

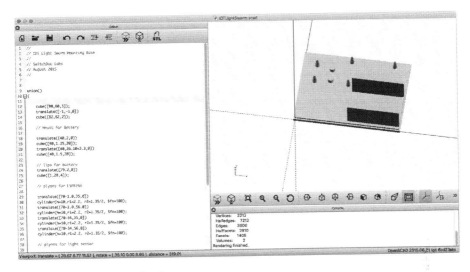

Figure 2-8. *OpenSCAD display*

As shown in Listing 2-1, the OpenSCAD programming code to build this stand is quite simple. It consists of cubes and cylinders of various sizes and types.

Listing 2-1. Mounting Base for the IOT LightSwarm

```
//
// IOT Light Swarm Mounting Base
//
// SwitchDoc Labs
// August 2015
//

union()
{

    cube([80,60,3]);
    translate([-1,-1,0])
    cube([82,62,2]);

    // Mount for Battery

    translate([40,2,0])
    cube([40,1.35,20]);
    translate([40,26.10+3.3,0])
    cube([40,1.5,20]);
```

```
  // lips for battery
  translate([79,2,0])
  cube([1,28,4]);

  // pylons for ESP8266

  translate([70-1.0,35,0])
  cylinder(h=10,r1=2.2, r2=1.35/2, $fn=100);
  translate([70-1.0,56,0])
  cylinder(h=10,r1=2.2, r2=1.35/2, $fn=100);
  translate([70-34,35,0])
  cylinder(h=10,r1=2.2, r2=1.35/2, $fn=100);
  translate([70-34,56,0])
  cylinder(h=10,r1=2.2, r2=1.35/2, $fn=100);

  // pylons for light sensor

  translate([10,35,0])
  cylinder(h=10,r1=2.2, r2=1.35/2, $fn=100);
  translate([10,49.5,0])
  cylinder(h=10,r1=2.2, r2=1.35/2, $fn=100);

 translate([22,37,0])
  cylinder(h=6,r1=2.2, r2=2.2, $fn=100);
  translate([22,47,0])
  cylinder(h=6,r1=2.2, r2=2.2, $fn=100);
}
```

You can see the completed stand and the FTDI cable in the upcoming Figure 2-9. Once designed, I quickly built five of them for the LightSwarm. Figure 2-10 shows a completed Swarm element.

The Full Wiring List

Table 2-3 provides the complete wiring list for a LightSwarm device. As you wire it, check off each wire for accuracy.

Table 2-3. *LightSwarm Wiring List*

From	To	Description
ESP8266 / GND	TCS34725 /GND	Ground for I2C Light Sensor
ESP8266 / 3V	TCS34725 / 3V3	3.3V Power for I2C Light Sensor
ESP8266 / #4	TCS34725 /SDA	SDA for I2C Light Sensor
ESP8266 / #5	TCS34725 /SCL	SCL for I2C Light Sensor
ESP8266 / GND	9VBat / "-" terminal (minus terminal)	Ground for battery
ESP8266 / VBat	9VBat / "+" terminal (plus 9V)	9V from battery
TCS34725 / LED	TCS34725 / INT	Connecting these two pins together allow for software control of bright LED on TCS34725 board

The FTDI cable is plugged into the end of the Adafruit Huzzah ESP8266. Make sure you align the black wire with the GND pin on the ESP8266 breakout board as in Figure 2-9. Figure 2-11 shows the fully complete LightSwarm device.

Figure 2-9. *FTDI Cable Plugged into ESP8266*

Figure 2-10. Completed LightSwarm Stand

Figure 2-11. A Complete LightSwarm Device

The Software

There are two major modules written for the LightSwarm. The first is ESP8266 code for the LightSwarm device itself (written in the Arduino IDE - written in simplified C and C++ language), and the second is the Raspberry Pi data-gathering software (written in Python on the Raspberry Pi).

The major design specifications for the LightSwarm Device software are the following:

- Device self discovery.
- Device becomes master when it has the brightest light; all others become slaves.
- Distributed voting method for determining master status.
- Self-organizing swarm. No server.
- Swarm must survive and recover from devices coming in and out of the network.
- Master device sends data to Raspberry Pi for analysis and distribution to Internet.

The entire code for the LightSwarm devices is provided in Listings 2-2 though 2-11 (with the exception of the TCS74725 light-sensor driver, available here [github.com/adafruit/Adafruit_TCS34725]). The code is also available on the APress web site [www.apress.com] and the SwitchDoc Labs github site [github.com/switchdoclabs/lightswarm].

Listing 2-2. LightSwarm Code

```
/*
Cooperative IOT Self Organizing Example
SwitchDoc Labs, August 2015

 */


#include <ESP8266WiFi.h>
#include <WiFiUdp.h>
#include <Wire.h>
#include "Adafruit_TCS34725.h"

#undef DEBUG

char ssid[] = "yyyyy";          // your wireless network SSID (name)
char pass[] = "xxxxxxx";        // your wireless network password

#define VERSIONNUMBER 28
```

```
#define SWARMSIZE 5
// 30 seconds is too old - it must be dead
#define SWARMTOOOLD 30000

int mySwarmID = 0;
```

Next in Listing 2-3, we define the necessary constants. Following are the definitions of all the Swarm Commands available:

- LIGHT_UPDATE_PACKET - Packet containing current light from a LightSwarm device. Used to determine who is master and who is slave;

- RESET_SWARM_PACKET - All LightSwarm devices are told to reset their software;

- CHANGE_TEST_PACKET - Designed to change the master / slave criteria (not implemented);

- RESET_ME_PACKET - Just reset a particular LightSwarm device ID;

- DEFINE_SERVER_LOGGER_PACKET - This is the new IP address of the Raspberry Pi so the LightSwarm device can send data packets;

- LOG_TO_SERVER_PACKET - Packets send from LightSwarm devices to Raspberry Pi;

- MASTER_CHANGE_PACKET - Packet sent from LightSwarm device when it becomes a master (not implemented);

- BLINK_BRIGHT_LED - Command to a LightSwarm device to blink the bright LED on the TCS34725.

After the constants in Listing 2-3, I set up the system variables for the devices. I am using UDP across the WiFi interface. What is UDP? UDP stands for User Datagram Protocol. UDP uses a simple connectionless model. Connectionless means that there is no handshake between the transmitting device and the receiving device to let the transmitter know that the receiver is actually there. Unlike TCP (Transmission Control Protocol), you have no idea or guarantee of data packets being delivered to any particular device. You can think of it as kind of a TV broadcast to your local network. Everyone gets it, but they don't have to read the packets. There are also subtle other effects – such as you don't have any guarantee that packets will arrive in the order they are sent. So why are we using UDP instead of TCP? I am using the broadcast mode of UDP so when a LightSwarm devices send out a message to the WiFi subnet, everybody gets it and if they are listening on the port 2910 (set above), then they can react to the message. This is how LightSwarm devices get discovered. Everybody starts sending packages (with random delays introduced) and all of the LightSwarm devices figure out who is present and who has the brightest light. Nothing in the LightSwarm system assigns IP numbers or names. They all figure it out themselves.

Listing 2-3. LightSwarm Constants

```
// Packet Types

#define LIGHT_UPDATE_PACKET 0
#define RESET_SWARM_PACKET 1
#define CHANGE_TEST_PACKET 2
#define RESET_ME_PACKET 3
#define DEFINE_SERVER_LOGGER_PACKET 4
#define LOG_TO_SERVER_PACKET 5
#define MASTER_CHANGE_PACKET 6
#define BLINK_BRIGHT_LED 7

unsigned int localPort = 2910;        // local port to listen for UDP packets

// master variables
boolean masterState = true;    // True if master, False if not
int swarmClear[SWARMSIZE];
int swarmVersion[SWARMSIZE];
int swarmState[SWARMSIZE];
long swarmTimeStamp[SWARMSIZE];    // for aging

IPAddress serverAddress = IPAddress(0, 0, 0, 0); // default no IP Address

int swarmAddresses[SWARMSIZE];   // Swarm addresses

// variables for light sensor

int clearColor;
int redColor;
int blueColor;
int greenColor;

const int PACKET_SIZE = 14; // Light Update Packet
const int BUFFERSIZE = 1024;

byte packetBuffer[BUFFERSIZE]; //buffer to hold incoming and outgoing
packets

// A UDP instance to let us send and receive packets over UDP
WiFiUDP udp;

/* Initialize with specific int time and gain values */
Adafruit_TCS34725 tcs = Adafruit_TCS34725(TCS34725_INTEGRATIONTIME_700MS,
TCS34725_GAIN_1X);

IPAddress localIP;
```

The setup() routine shown in Listing 2-4 is only run once after reset of the ESP8266 and is used to set up all the devices and print logging information to the Serial port on the ESP8266, where, if you have the FTDI cable connected, you can see the logging information and debugging information on your PC or Mac.

Listing 2-4. The Setup() Function for LightSwarm

```
void setup()
{

  Serial.begin(115200);
  Serial.println();
  Serial.println();

  Serial.println("");
  Serial.println("--------------------------");
  Serial.println("LightSwarm");
  Serial.print("Version ");
  Serial.println(VERSIONNUMBER);
  Serial.println("--------------------------");

  Serial.println(F(" 09/03/2015"));
  Serial.print(F("Compiled at:"));
  Serial.print (F(__TIME__));
  Serial.print(F(" "));
  Serial.println(F(__DATE__));
  Serial.println();
  pinMode(0, OUTPUT);

  digitalWrite(0, LOW);
  delay(500);
  digitalWrite(0, HIGH);
```

Here we use the floating value of the analog input on the ESP8266 to set the pseudo-random number generation seed. This will vary a bit from device to device, and so it's not a bad way of initializing the pseudo-random number generator. If you put a fixed number as the argument, it will always generate the same set of pseudo-random numbers. This can be very useful in testing. Listing 2-5 shows the setup of the random seed and the detection of the TCS34725.

What is a pseudo-random number generator? It is an algorithm for generating a sequence of numbers whose properties approximate a truly random number sequence. It is not a truly random sequence of numbers, but it is close. Good enough for our usage.

Listing 2-5. Remainder of the Setup() Function for LightSwarm

```
randomSeed(analogRead(A0));
  Serial.print("analogRead(A0)=");
  Serial.println(analogRead(A0));

  if (tcs.begin()) {
    Serial.println("Found sensor");
  } else {
    Serial.println("No TCS34725 found ... check your connections");

  }

  // turn off the light
  tcs.setInterrupt(true);   // true means off, false means on

  // everybody starts at 0 and changes from there
  mySwarmID = 0;

  // We start by connecting to a WiFi network
  Serial.print("LightSwarm Instance: ");
  Serial.println(mySwarmID);

  Serial.print("Connecting to ");
  Serial.println(ssid);
  WiFi.begin(ssid, pass);

  // initialize Swarm Address - we start out as swarmID of 0

  while (WiFi.status() != WL_CONNECTED) {
    delay(500);
    Serial.print(".");
  }
  Serial.println("");

  Serial.println("WiFi connected");
  Serial.println("IP address: ");
  Serial.println(WiFi.localIP());

  Serial.println("Starting UDP");

  udp.begin(localPort);
  Serial.print("Local port: ");
  Serial.println(udp.localPort());
```

```
// initialize light sensor and arrays
int i;
for (i = 0; i < SWARMSIZE; i++)
{

  swarmAddresses[i] = 0;
  swarmClear[i] = 0;
  swarmTimeStamp[i] = -1;
}
swarmClear[mySwarmID] = 0;
swarmTimeStamp[mySwarmID] = 1;    // I am always in time to myself
clearColor = swarmClear[mySwarmID];
swarmVersion[mySwarmID] = VERSIONNUMBER;
swarmState[mySwarmID] = masterState;
Serial.print("clearColor =");
Serial.println(clearColor);
```

Now we have initialized all the data structures for describing our LightSwarm device and the states of the light sensor. Listing 2-6 sets the SwarmID based on the current device IP address. When you turn on a LightSwarm device and it connects to a WiFi access point, the access point assigns a unique IP address to the LightSwarm device. This is done through a process called DHCP (Dynamic Host Configuration Protocol) [en.wikipedia.org/wiki/Dynamic_Host_Configuration_Protocol]. While the number will be different for each LightSwarm device, it is not random. Typically, if you power a specific device down and power it up again, the access point will assign the same IP address. However, you can't count on this. The access point knows your specific device because each and every WiFi interface has a specific and unique MAC (Media Access Control) number, which is usually never changed.

▨ **SwitchDoc Note**   Faking MAC addresses allows you to impersonate other devices with your device in some cases, and you can use MAC addresses to track specific machines by looking at the network. This is why Apple, Inc. has started using random MAC addresses in their devices while scanning for networks. If random MAC addresses aren't used, then researchers have confirmed that it is possible to link a specific real identity to a particular wireless MAC address [Cunche, Mathieu. "I know your MAC Address: Targeted tracking of individual using Wi-Fi". *2013*].

Listing 2-6. Setting the SwarmID from IP Address

```
// set SwarmID based on IP address

localIP = WiFi.localIP();

swarmAddresses[0] = localIP[3];

mySwarmID = 0;

Serial.print("MySwarmID=");
Serial.println(mySwarmID);

}
```

The second main section of the LightSwarm device code is the loop(). The loop() function does precisely what its name suggests and loops infinitely, allowing your program to change and respond. This is the section of the code that performs the main work of the LightSwarm code.

```
void loop()
{
  int secondsCount;
  int lastSecondsCount;

  lastSecondsCount = 0;
#define LOGHOWOFTEN

  secondsCount = millis() / 100;
```

In this Listing 2-7, we read all the data from the TCS34725 sensor to find out how bright the ambient light currently is. This forms the substance of the data to determine who the master in the swarm is.

After the delay (300) line in Listing 2-7, I check for UDP packets being broadcast to port 2910. Remember the way the swarm is using UDP is in broadcast mode and all packets are being received by everybody all the time. Note, this sets a limit of how many swarm devices you can have (limited to the subnet size) and also by the congestion of having too many messages go through at the same time. This was pretty easy to simulate by increasing the rate that packets are sent. The swarm still functions but the behavior becomes more erratic and with sometimes large delays.

Listing 2-7. Reading the Light Color

```
uint16_t r, g, b, c, colorTemp, lux;

tcs.getRawData(&r, &g, &b, &c);
colorTemp = tcs.calculateColorTemperature(r, g, b);
lux = tcs.calculateLux(r, g, b);

Serial.print("Color Temp: "); Serial.print(colorTemp, DEC); Serial.
print(" K - ");
Serial.print("Lux: "); Serial.print(lux, DEC); Serial.print(" - ");
Serial.print("R: "); Serial.print(r, DEC); Serial.print(" ");
Serial.print("G: "); Serial.print(g, DEC); Serial.print(" ");
Serial.print("B: "); Serial.print(b, DEC); Serial.print(" ");
Serial.print("C: "); Serial.print(c, DEC); Serial.print(" ");
Serial.println(" ");

clearColor = c;
redColor = r;
blueColor = b;
greenColor = g;

swarmClear[mySwarmID] = clearColor;

// wait to see if a reply is available
delay(300);

int cb = udp.parsePacket();

if (!cb) {
  //  Serial.println("no packet yet");
  Serial.print(".");
}
else {
```

In Listing 2-8, we interpret all the packets depending on the packet type.

Listing 2-8. Interpreting the Packet Type

```
// We've received a packet, read the data from it

   udp.read(packetBuffer, PACKET_SIZE); // read the packet into the buffer
   Serial.print("packetbuffer[1] =");
   Serial.println(packetBuffer[1]);
   if (packetBuffer[1] == LIGHT_UPDATE_PACKET)
```

```
{
  Serial.print("LIGHT_UPDATE_PACKET received from LightSwarm #");
  Serial.println(packetBuffer[2]);
  setAndReturnMySwarmIndex(packetBuffer[2]);

  Serial.print("LS Packet Recieved from #");
  Serial.print(packetBuffer[2]);
  Serial.print(" SwarmState:");
  if (packetBuffer[3] == 0)
    Serial.print("SLAVE");
  else
    Serial.print("MASTER");
  Serial.print(" CC:");
  Serial.print(packetBuffer[5] * 256 + packetBuffer[6]);
  Serial.print(" RC:");
  Serial.print(packetBuffer[7] * 256 + packetBuffer[8]);
  Serial.print(" GC:");
  Serial.print(packetBuffer[9] * 256 + packetBuffer[10]);
  Serial.print(" BC:");
  Serial.print(packetBuffer[11] * 256 + packetBuffer[12]);
  Serial.print(" Version=");
  Serial.println(packetBuffer[4]);

  // record the incoming clear color

  swarmClear[setAndReturnMySwarmIndex(packetBuffer[2])] = packetBuffer[5]
  * 256 + packetBuffer[6];
  swarmVersion[setAndReturnMySwarmIndex(packetBuffer[2])] =
  packetBuffer[4];
  swarmState[setAndReturnMySwarmIndex(packetBuffer[2])] =
  packetBuffer[3];
  swarmTimeStamp[setAndReturnMySwarmIndex(packetBuffer[2])] = millis();

  // Check to see if I am master!
  checkAndSetIfMaster();

}
```

The RESET_SWARM_PACKET command sets all of the LightSwarm devices to master (turning on the red LED on each) and then lets the LightSwarm software vote and determine who has the brightest light. As each device receives a LIGHT_UPDATE_ PACKET, it compares the light from that swarm device to its own sensor and becomes a slave if their light is brighter. Eventually, the swarm figures out who has the brightest light. I have been sending this periodically from the Raspberry Pi and watching the devices work it out. It makes an interesting video. Listing 2-9 shows how LightSwarm interprets incoming packets. The very last section of Listing 2-9 shows how the Swarm element updates everybody else in the Swarm what is going on with this device and then we send a data packet to the Raspberry Pi if we are the swarm master.

Listing 2-9. LightSwarm Packet Interpretation Code

```
if (packetBuffer[1] == RESET_SWARM_PACKET)
{
  Serial.println(">>>>>>>>RESET_SWARM_PACKETPacket Received");
  masterState = true;
  Serial.println("Reset Swarm:  I just BECAME Master (and everybody
  else!)");
  digitalWrite(0, LOW);

}

if (packetBuffer[1] == CHANGE_TEST_PACKET)
{
  Serial.println(">>>>>>>>CHANGE_TEST_PACKET Packet Received");
  Serial.println("not implemented");
  int i;
  for (i = 0; i < PACKET_SIZE; i++)
  {
    if (i == 2)
    {
      Serial.print("LPS[");
      Serial.print(i);
      Serial.print("] = ");
      Serial.println(packetBuffer[i]);

    }
    else
    {
      Serial.print("LPS[");
      Serial.print(i);
      Serial.print("] = 0x");
      Serial.println(packetBuffer[i], HEX);
    }

  }

}

if (packetBuffer[1] == RESET_ME_PACKET)
{
  Serial.println(">>>>>>>>>RESET_ME_PACKET Packet Received");
```

```
  if (packetBuffer[2] == swarmAddresses[mySwarmID])
  {
    masterState = true;
    Serial.println("Reset Me:  I just BECAME Master");
    digitalWrite(0, LOW);

  }
  else
  {
    Serial.print("Wanted #");
    Serial.print(packetBuffer[2]);
    Serial.println(" Not me - reset ignored");
  }

}

}

if (packetBuffer[1] ==  DEFINE_SERVER_LOGGER_PACKET)
{
  Serial.println(">>>>>>>>>DEFINE_SERVER_LOGGER_PACKET Packet Received");
  serverAddress = IPAddress(packetBuffer[4], packetBuffer[5],
  packetBuffer[6], packetBuffer[7]);
  Serial.print("Server address received: ");
  Serial.println(serverAddress);

}
if (packetBuffer[1] ==  BLINK_BRIGHT_LED)
{
  Serial.println(">>>>>>>>>BLINK_BRIGHT_LED Packet Received");
  if (packetBuffer[2] == swarmAddresses[mySwarmID])
  {

    tcs.setInterrupt(false);  // true means off, false means on
    delay(packetBuffer[4] * 100);
    tcs.setInterrupt(true);  // true means off, false means on
  }
  else
  {
    Serial.print("Wanted #");
    Serial.print(packetBuffer[2]);
    Serial.println(" Not me - reset ignored");
  }

}
```

```
Serial.print("MasterStatus:");
if (masterState == true)
{
  digitalWrite(0, LOW);
  Serial.print("MASTER");
}
else
{
  digitalWrite(0, HIGH);
  Serial.print("SLAVE");
}
  Serial.print("/cc=");
  Serial.print(clearColor);
  Serial.print("/KS:");
  Serial.println(serverAddress);

  Serial.println("--------");

  int i;
  for (i = 0; i < SWARMSIZE; i++)
{
  Serial.print("swarmAddress[");
  Serial.print(i);
  Serial.print("] = ");
  Serial.println(swarmAddresses[i]);
}
  Serial.println("--------");

  broadcastARandomUpdatePacket();
  sendLogToServer();

} // end of loop()
```

Listing 2-10 is used to send out light packets to a swarm address. Although a specific address is allowed by this function, we set the last octet of the IP address (201 in the IP address 192.168.1.201) in the calling function to 255, which is the UDP broadcast address.

Listing 2-10. Broadcasting to the Swarm

```
// send an LIGHT Packet request to the swarms at the given address
unsigned long sendLightUpdatePacket(IPAddress & address)
{

  // set all bytes in the buffer to 0
  memset(packetBuffer, 0, PACKET_SIZE);
  // Initialize values needed to form Light Packet
  // (see URL above for details on the packets)
  packetBuffer[0] = 0xF0;    // StartByte
```

```
packetBuffer[1] = LIGHT_UPDATE_PACKET;      // Packet Type
packetBuffer[2] = localIP[3];      // Sending Swarm Number
packetBuffer[3] = masterState;  // 0 = slave, 1 = master
packetBuffer[4] = VERSIONNUMBER;  // Software Version
packetBuffer[5] = (clearColor & 0xFF00) >> 8; // Clear High Byte
packetBuffer[6] = (clearColor & 0x00FF); // Clear Low Byte
packetBuffer[7] = (redColor & 0xFF00) >> 8; // Red High Byte
packetBuffer[8] = (redColor & 0x00FF); // Red Low Byte
packetBuffer[9] = (greenColor & 0xFF00) >> 8; // green High Byte
packetBuffer[10] = (greenColor & 0x00FF); // green Low Byte
packetBuffer[11] = (blueColor & 0xFF00) >> 8; // blue High Byte
packetBuffer[12] = (blueColor & 0x00FF); // blue Low Byte
packetBuffer[13] = 0x0F;   //End Byte

// all Light Packet fields have been given values, now
// you can send a packet requesting coordination
udp.beginPacketMulticast(address,  localPort, WiFi.localIP()); //
udp.write(packetBuffer, PACKET_SIZE);
udp.endPacket();
}

// delay 0-MAXDELAY seconds
#define MAXDELAY 500

void broadcastARandomUpdatePacket()
{

  int sendToLightSwarm = 255;
  Serial.print("Broadcast ToSwarm = ");
  Serial.print(sendToLightSwarm);
  Serial.print(" ");

  // delay 0-MAXDELAY seconds
  int randomDelay;
  randomDelay = random(0, MAXDELAY);
  Serial.print("Delay = ");
  Serial.print(randomDelay);
  Serial.print("ms : ");

  delay(randomDelay);

  IPAddress sendSwarmAddress(192, 168, 1, sendToLightSwarm); // my Swarm
  Address
  sendLightUpdatePacket(sendSwarmAddress);

}
```

In the function in Listing 2-11, I check if we just became master and also update the status of all the LightSwarm devices. This is where the timeout function is implemented that will remove stale or dead devices from the swarm.

Listing 2-11. Master Check and Update

```
void checkAndSetIfMaster()
{

  int i;
  for (i = 0; i < SWARMSIZE; i++)
  {

#ifdef DEBUG

    Serial.print("swarmClear[");
    Serial.print(i);
    Serial.print("] = ");
    Serial.print(swarmClear[i]);
    Serial.print("  swarmTimeStamp[");
    Serial.print(i);
    Serial.print("] = ");
    Serial.println(swarmTimeStamp[i]);
#endif

    Serial.print("#");
    Serial.print(i);
    Serial.print("/");
    Serial.print(swarmState[i]);
    Serial.print("/");
    Serial.print(swarmVersion[i]);
    Serial.print(":");
    // age data
    int howLongAgo = millis() - swarmTimeStamp[i] ;

    if (swarmTimeStamp[i] == 0)
    {
      Serial.print("TO ");
    }
    else if (swarmTimeStamp[i] == -1)
    {
      Serial.print("NP ");
    }
    else if (swarmTimeStamp[i] == 1)
    {
      Serial.print("ME ");
    }
```

```
  else if (howLongAgo > SWARMTOOOLD)
  {
    Serial.print("TO ");
    swarmTimeStamp[i] = 0;
    swarmClear[i] = 0;

  }
  else
  {
    Serial.print("PR ");

  }
}

Serial.println();
boolean setMaster = true;

for (i = 0; i < SWARMSIZE; i++)
{

  if (swarmClear[mySwarmID] >= swarmClear[i])
  {
    // I might be master!

  }
  else
  {
    // nope, not master
    setMaster = false;
    break;
  }

}
if (setMaster == true)
{
  if (masterState == false)
  {
    Serial.println("I just BECAME Master");
    digitalWrite(0, LOW);
  }

  masterState = true;
}
```

```
  else
  {
    if (masterState == true)
    {
      Serial.println("I just LOST Master");
      digitalWrite(0, HIGH);
    }

    masterState = false;
  }

  swarmState[mySwarmID] = masterState;

}

int setAndReturnMySwarmIndex(int incomingID)
{

  int i;
  for (i = 0; i< SWARMSIZE; i++)
  {
    if (swarmAddresses[i] == incomingID)
    {
      return i;
    }
    else
    if (swarmAddresses[i] == 0)  // not in the system, so put it in
    {

      swarmAddresses[i] = incomingID;
      Serial.print("incomingID ");
      Serial.print(incomingID);
      Serial.print("  assigned #");
      Serial.println(i);
      return i;
    }

  }

  // if we get here, then we have a new swarm member.
  // Delete the oldest swarm member and add the new one in
  // (this will probably be the one that dropped out)
```

```
 int oldSwarmID;
 long oldTime;
 oldTime = millis();
 for (i = 0;  i < SWARMSIZE; i++)
{
 if (oldTime > swarmTimeStamp[i])
 {
   oldTime = swarmTimeStamp[i];
   oldSwarmID = i;
 }

}

// remove the old one and put this one in....
swarmAddresses[oldSwarmID] = incomingID;
// the rest will be filled in by Light Packet Receive

}

// send log packet to Server if master and server address defined

void sendLogToServer()
{

  // build the string

  char myBuildString[1000];
  myBuildString[0] = '\0';

  if (masterState == true)
  {
    // now check for server address defined
    if ((serverAddress[0] == 0) && (serverAddress[1] == 0))
    {
      return;  // we are done.  not defined
    }
    else
    {
      // now send the packet as a string with the following format:
      // swarmID, MasterSlave, SoftwareVersion, clearColor, Status | ....
      next Swarm ID
      // 0,1,15,3883, PR | 1,0,14,399, PR | ....

      int i;
      char swarmString[20];
      swarmString[0] = '\0';
```

```
    for (i = 0; i < SWARMSIZE; i++)
    {

      char stateString[5];
      stateString[0] = '\0';
      if (swarmTimeStamp[i] == 0)
      {
        strcat(stateString, "TO");
      }
      else if (swarmTimeStamp[i] == -1)
      {
        strcat(stateString, "NP");
      }
      else if (swarmTimeStamp[i] == 1)
      {
        strcat(stateString, "PR");
      }
      else
      {
        strcat(stateString, "PR");
      }

      sprintf(swarmString, " %i,%i,%i,%i,%s,%i ", i, swarmState[i],
      swarmVersion[i], swarmClear[i], stateString, swarmAddresses[i]);

      strcat(myBuildString, swarmString);
      if (i < SWARMSIZE - 1)
      {

        strcat(myBuildString, "|");

      }
    }

}

// set all bytes in the buffer to 0
memset(packetBuffer, 0, BUFFERSIZE);
// Initialize values needed to form Light Packet
// (see URL above for details on the packets)
packetBuffer[0] = 0xF0;    // StartByte
packetBuffer[1] = LOG_TO_SERVER_PACKET;      // Packet Type
packetBuffer[2] = localIP[3];      // Sending Swarm Number
packetBuffer[3] = strlen(myBuildString); // length of string in bytes
packetBuffer[4] = VERSIONNUMBER;   // Software Version
int i;
```

```
for (i = 0; i < strlen(myBuildString); i++)
{
  packetBuffer[i + 5] = myBuildString[i];// first string byte
}

packetBuffer[i + 5] = 0x0F; //End Byte
Serial.print("Sending Log to Sever:");
Serial.println(myBuildString);
int packetLength;
packetLength = i + 5 + 1;

udp.beginPacket(serverAddress,  localPort); //

udp.write(packetBuffer, packetLength);
udp.endPacket();

}

}
```

That is the entire LightSwarm device code. When compiling this code on the Arduino IDE targeting the Adafruit ESP8266, we get the following:

Sketch uses 308,736 bytes (29%) of program storage space. Maximum is 1,044,464 bytes.

Global variables use 50,572 bytes (61%) of dynamic memory, leaving 31,348 bytes for local variables. Maximum is 81,920 bytes.

Still a lot of space left for more code. Most of the compiled codes space above are used by the system libraries for WiFi and running the ESP8266.

Self-Organizing Behavior

Why do we say that the LightSwarm code is self-organizing? It is because there is no central control of who is the master and who is the slave. This makes the system more reliable and able to function even in a bad environment. Self-organization is defined as a process where some sort of order arises out of the local interactions between smaller items in an initially disordered system.

Typically these kinds of systems are robust and able to survive in a chaotic environment. Self-organizing systems occur in a variety of physical, biological, and social systems.

One reason to build these kinds of systems is that the individual devices can be small and not very smart, and yet the overall task or picture of the data being collected and processed can be amazingly interesting and informative.

Monitoring and Debugging the System with the Raspberry Pi (the Smart Guy on the Block)

The Raspberry Pi is used in LightSwarm primarily as a data storage device for examining the LightSwarm data and telling what is going on in the swarm. You can send a few commands to reset the swarm, turn lights on, etc., but the swarm runs itself with or without the Raspberry Pi running. However, debugging self-organizing systems like this are difficult without some way of watching what is going on with the swarm, preferably from another computer. And that is what we have done with the LightSwarm Logger software on the Raspberry Pi. The primary design criteria for this software follows:

- Read and log information on the swarm behavior.

- Reproduce archival swarm behavior.

- Provide methods for testing swarm behavior (such as resetting the swarm).

- Provide real-time information to the Internet on swarm behavior and status.

Remember that the Raspberry Pi is a full, complex, and powerful computer system that goes way beyond what you can do with an ESP8266. First we will look at the LightSwarm logging software and then the software that supports the RasPiConnect LightSwarm panel. Note that we are not storing the information coming from the swarm devices in this software, but we could easily add logging software that would populate a MySQL database that would allow us to store and analyze the information coming in from the swarm.

LightSwarm Logging Software Written in Python

The entire code base of the LightSwarm Logging software is available off the APress site [APress code site] and on the SwitchDoc Labs github site [`github.com/switchdoclabs/lightswarm_Pi`]. I am picking out the most interesting code in the Logging software to comment on and explain.

First of all, this program is written in Python. Python is a widely used programming language, especially with Raspberry Pi coders. There are a number of device libraries available for building your own IOT devices and there is even a small version that runs on the ESP8266. Python's design philosophy emphasizes code readability. Indenting is important in Python, so keep that in mind as you look at the code below.

■ **SwitchDoc Note**   Python is "weakly typed" meaning you define a variable and the type by the first time you use it. Some programmers like this, but I don't. Misspelling a variable name makes a whole new variable and can cause great confusion. My prejudice is toward "strongly typed" languages as it tends to reduce the number of coding errors, at the cost of having to think about and declare variables explicitly.

The first section of this program defines all the needed libraries (import statements) and defines necessary "constants." Python does not have a way to define constants, so you declare variables for constant values, which by my convention are all in uppercase. There are other ways of defining constants by using classes and functions, but they are more complex than just defining another variable. Listing 2-13 shows how the variables and constants are initialized.

Listing 2-13. Import and Constant Value Declaration

```
'''
    LightSwarm Raspberry Pi Logger
    SwitchDoc Labs
    September 2015
'''


import sys
import time
import random

from netifaces import interfaces, ifaddresses, AF_INET

from socket import *

VERSIONNUMBER = 6
# packet type definitions
LIGHT_UPDATE_PACKET = 0
RESET_SWARM_PACKET = 1
CHANGE_TEST_PACKET = 2     # Not Implemented
RESET_ME_PACKET = 3
DEFINE_SERVER_LOGGER_PACKET = 4
LOG_TO_SERVER_PACKET = 5
MASTER_CHANGE_PACKET = 6
BLINK_BRIGHT_LED = 7

MYPORT = 2910

SWARMSIZE = 5
```

Listing 2-14 defines the interface between the LightSwarm Logging software and the RasPiConnect control panel software [www.milocreek.com]. The author wrote a tutorial about this command-passing structure in *MagPi* magazine reprinted on the SwitchDoc Labs web site [www.switchdoc.com/2014/07/build-control-panels-tutorial-raspiconnect/]. These are the three important functions:

- processCommand(s) - When a command is received from the RasPiConnect server software running on the same computer, this function defines all the actions to be completed when a specific command is received from RasPiConnect.

- completeCommandWithValue(value) - call function and return a value to RasPiConnect when you have completed a command.

- completeCommand() - call function when you have completed a command to tell RasPiConnect you are done with the command.

Basically, the idea is that when you ask for a data refresh or push a button on the RasPiConnect control panel, the RasPiConnect server software sends a command to the LightSwarm logging software that is running on a different thread in the same system. Remember that the Raspberry Pi Linux-based system is multitasking and you can run many different programs at once.

Listing 2-14. RaspiConnect Code

```
logString = ""
# command from RasPiConnect Execution Code

def completeCommand():

        f = open("/home/pi/LightSwarm/state/LSCommand.txt", "w")
        f.write("DONE")
        f.close()

def completeCommandWithValue(value):

        f = open("/home/pi/LightSwarm/state/LSResponse.txt", "w")
        f.write(value)
        print "in completeCommandWithValue=", value
        f.close()

        completeCommand()

def processCommand(s):
        f = open("//home/pi/LightSwarm/state/LSCommand.txt", "r")
        command = f.read()
        f.close()

        if (command == "") or (command == "DONE"):
                # Nothing to do
                return False

        # Check for our commands

        print "Processing Command: ", command
        if (command == "STATUS"):

                completeCommandWithValue(logString)

                return True
```

```
if (command == "RESETSWARM"):

        SendRESET_SWARM_PACKET(s)

        completeCommand()

        return True

# check for , commands

print "command=%s" % command
myCommandList = command.split(',')
print "myCommandList=", myCommandList

if (myCommandList.count > 1):
        # we have a list command

        if (myCommandList[0]== "BLINKLIGHT"):
                SendBLINK_BRIGHT_LED(s, int(myCommandList[1]), 1)

        if (myCommandList[0]== "RESETSELECTED"):
                SendRESET_ME_PACKET(s, int(myCommandList[1]))

        if (myCommandList[0]== "SENDSERVER"):
                SendDEFINE_SERVER_LOGGER_PACKET(s)

        completeCommand()

        return True

completeCommand()

return False
```

In Listing 2-15, I have the actual LightSwarm command implementations for sending packets. Listing 2-15 just shows the first packet type to illustrate the concepts.

Listing 2-15. Light Swam Command Packet Definitions

```
# UDP Commands and packets

def SendDEFINE_SERVER_LOGGER_PACKET(s):
        print "DEFINE_SERVER_LOGGER_PACKET Sent"
        s.setsockopt(SOL_SOCKET, SO_BROADCAST, 1)
```

```
# get IP address
for ifaceName in interfaces():
            addresses = [i['addr'] for i in ifaddresses(ifaceName).
            setdefault(AF_INET, [{'addr':'No IP addr'}] )]
            print '%s: %s' % (ifaceName, ', '.join(addresses))

# last interface (wlan0) grabbed
print addresses
myIP = addresses[0].split('.')
print myIP
data= ["" for i in range(14)]

data[0] = chr(0xF0)
data[1] = chr(DEFINE_SERVER_LOGGER_PACKET)
data[2] = chr(0xFF) # swarm id (FF means not part of swarm)
data[3] = chr(VERSIONNUMBER)
data[4] = chr(int(myIP[0])) # first octet of ip
data[5] = chr(int(myIP[1])) # second octet of ip
data[6] = chr(int(myIP[2])) # third octet of ip
data[7] = chr(int(myIP[3])) # fourth octet of ip
data[8] = chr(0x00)
data[9] = chr(0x00)
data[10] = chr(0x00)
data[11] = chr(0x00)
data[12] = chr(0x00)
data[13] = chr(0x0F)


        s.sendto(''.join(data), ('<broadcast>', MYPORT))
```

The next section of the code to be discussed is the web map that is used by the
RasPiConnect web control to display HTML code. The code in Listing 2-16 produces
Figure 2-12.

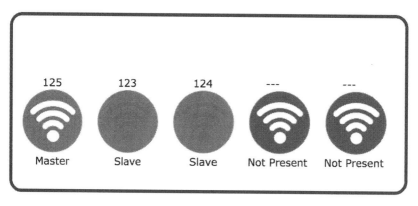

Figure 2-12. *HTML Web Control in RasPiConnect Produced by Web Map Code in
LightSwarm Logging Software*

Listing 2-16. Web page Building Code

```
# build Webmap

def buildWebMapToFile(logString, swarmSize ):

        f = open("/home/pi/RasPiConnectServer/Templates/W-1a.txt", "w")

    webresponse = ""

    swarmList = logString.split("|")
    for i in range(0,swarmSize):
        swarmElement = swarmList[i].split(",")
        print "swarmElement=", swarmElement
        webresponse += "<figure>"
        webresponse += "<figcaption"
        webresponse += " style='position: absolute; top: "
        webresponse +=  str(100-20)
        webresponse +=  "px; left: "
        +str(20+120*i)+  "px;'/>\n"
        if (int(swarmElement[5]) == 0):
                webresponse += "    &nb
                sp;---"
        else:
                webresponse += "    &nbs
                p; %s" % swarmElement[5]

        webresponse += "</figcaption>"
        webresponse += "<img src='" + "192.168.1.40:9750"

        if (swarmElement[4] == "PR"):
                if (swarmElement[1] == "1"):
                        webresponse += "/static/On-Master.png'
                        style='position: absolute; top: "
                else:
                        webresponse += "/static/On-Slave.png'
                        style='position: absolute; top: "
        else:
                if (swarmElement[4] == "TO"):
                        webresponse += "/static/Off-TimeOut.
                        png' style='position: absolute; top: "
```

```
                                    else:
                                        webresponse += "/static/Off-
                                        NotPresent.png' style='position:
                                        absolute; top: "

                            webresponse +=  str(100)
                            webresponse +=  "px; left: "
                            +str(20+120*i)+  "px;'/>\n"

                            webresponse +=  "<figcaption"
                            webresponse +=  " style='position: absolute; top: "
                            webresponse +=  str(100+100)
                            webresponse +=  "px; left: "
                            +str(20+120*i)+  "px;'/>\n"
                            if (swarmElement[4] == "PR"):
                                    if (swarmElement[1] == "1"):
                                        webresponse += "   &
                                        nbsp;Master"
                                        else:
                                        webresponse += "   &n
                                        bsp; Slave"
                            else:
                                    if (swarmElement[4] == "TO"):
                                            webresponse += "TimeOut"
                                    else:
                                            webresponse += "Not Present"

                            webresponse += "</figcaption>"

                            webresponse += "</figure>"

                #print webresponse
                f.write(webresponse)

                f.close()
```

Listing 2-17 looks at incoming swarm IDs and builds a current table of matching IDs, removing old ones when adding new ones. The maximum number of swarm devices you can have is five, but can be easily increased.

Listing 2-17. Incoming Swarm Analysis Code

```
def setAndReturnSwarmID(incomingID):

        for i in range(0,SWARMSIZE):
              if (swarmStatus[i][5] == incomingID):
                            return i
                    else:
                        if (swarmStatus[i][5] == 0):  # not in the system,
                        so put it in

                                    swarmStatus[i][5] = incomingID;
                                    print "incomingID %d " % incomingID
                                    print "assigned #%d" % i
                                    return i

        # if we get here, then we have a new swarm member.
        # Delete the oldest swarm member and add the new one in
        # (this will probably be the one that dropped out)

        oldTime = time.time();
        oldSwarmID = 0
        for i in range(0,SWARMSIZE):
                  if (oldTime > swarmStatus[i][1]):
                            oldTime = swarmStatus[i][1]
                            oldSwarmID = i

        # remove the old one and put this one in....
         swarmStatus[oldSwarmID][5] = incomingID;
         # the rest will be filled in by Light Packet Receive
        print "oldSwarmID %i" % oldSwarmID

        return oldSwarmID
```

Finally, Listing 2-18 is the main code for the Python program. It is very similar in function to the setup() code for the ESP8266 in the Arduino IDE. We use this to define variables, send out one-time commands, and set up the UDP interface.

Listing 2-18. LightSwarm Logger Startup Code

```
# set up sockets for UDP

s=socket(AF_INET, SOCK_DGRAM)
host = 'localhost';
s.bind(('',MYPORT))
```

```
print "--------------"
print "LightSwarm Logger"
print "Version ", VERSIONNUMBER
print "-------------"

# first send out DEFINE_SERVER_LOGGER_PACKET to tell swarm where to send
logging information

SendDEFINE_SERVER_LOGGER_PACKET(s)
time.sleep(3)
SendDEFINE_SERVER_LOGGER_PACKET(s)

# swarmStatus
swarmStatus = [[0 for x  in range(6)] for x in range(SWARMSIZE)]

# 6 items per swarm item

# 0 - NP  Not present, P = present, TO = time out
# 1 - timestamp of last LIGHT_UPDATE_PACKET received
# 2 - Master or slave status   M S
# 3 - Current Test Item - 0 - CC 1 - Lux 2 - Red 3 - Green  4 - Blue
# 4 - Current Test Direction  0 >=   1 <=
# 5 - IP Address of Swarm

for i in range(0,SWARMSIZE):
        swarmStatus[i][0] = "NP"
        swarmStatus[i][5] = 0

#300 seconds round
seconds_300_round = time.time() + 300.0

#120 seconds round
seconds_120_round = time.time() + 120.0

completeCommand() # ie RasPiConnect System - clear out old commands
```

Listing 2-19 provides the main program loop. Note this is very similar to the loop() function in the ESP8266. In this code, we check for incoming UDP packets, process RasPiConnect commands, update status information, and perform periodic commands. It is in this loop that we would be storing the Swarm status, packets, and information if we wanted to reproduce the swarm behavior archivally.

Listing 2-19. Raspberry Pi Logger Main Loop

```
while(1) :

        # receive datclient (data, addr)
        d = s.recvfrom(1024)

        message = d[0]
        addr = d[1]
        if (len(message) == 14):
                if (ord(message[1]) == LIGHT_UPDATE_PACKET):
                    incomingSwarmID = setAndReturnSwarmID(ord(message[2]))
                    swarmStatus[incomingSwarmID][0] = "P"
                    swarmStatus[incomingSwarmID][1] = time.time()

                if (ord(message[1]) == RESET_SWARM_PACKET):
                    print "Swarm RESET_SWARM_PACKET Received"
                    print "received from addr:",addr

                if (ord(message[1]) == CHANGE_TEST_PACKET):
                    print "Swarm CHANGE_TEST_PACKET Received"
                    print "received from addr:",addr

                if (ord(message[1]) == RESET_ME_PACKET):
                    print "Swarm RESET_ME_PACKET Received"
                    print "received from addr:",addr

                if (ord(message[1]) == DEFINE_SERVER_LOGGER_PACKET):
                    print "Swarm DEFINE_SERVER_LOGGER_PACKET Received"
                    print "received from addr:",addr

                if (ord(message[1]) == MASTER_CHANGE_PACKET):
                    print "Swarm MASTER_CHANGE_PACKET Received"
                    print "received from addr:",addr

                    for i in range(0,14):
                            print "ls["+str(i)+"]="+format(ord(message
                            [i]), "#04x")
        else:
                if (ord(message[1]) == LOG_TO_SERVER_PACKET):
                        print "Swarm LOG_TO_SERVER_PACKET Received"

                        # process the Log Packet
                        logString = parseLogPacket(message)
                        buildWebMapToFile(logString, SWARMSIZE )

                else:
                        print "error message length = ",len(message)
```

```
if (time.time() >  seconds_120_round):
        # do our 2 minute round
        print ">>>>doing 120 second task"
        sendTo = random.randint(0,SWARMSIZE-1)
        SendBLINK_BRIGHT_LED(s, sendTo, 1)
        seconds_120_round = time.time() + 120.0

if (time.time() >  seconds_300_round):
        # do our 2 minute round
        print ">>>>doing 300 second task"
        SendDEFINE_SERVER_LOGGER_PACKET(s)
        seconds_300_round = time.time() + 300.0

processCommand(s)

#print swarmStatus
```

Next, I will look at parts of the RasPiConnect Server code.

The RasPiConnect Control Panel in Real Time

RasPiConnect (and the Arduino version, ArduinoConnect) is software designed for the iPad and iPhone for building Internet-enabled control panels connecting to small computers. It is designed to be light in memory and processor usage. It has prebuilt servers in Python for the Raspberry Pi (actually any type of computer running Python) and in C/C++ for use in the Arduino IDE. We could easily implement a version running on the EPS8266 and plan to do that in a future project. You can do complex interface designs using RasPiConnect. Consider the screen in Figure 2-13 showing one of six screens used in ProjectCuracao, a massive environmental sensing solar-powered project running remotely on the Caribbean island of Curacao [www.switchdoc.com/project-curacao-introduction-part-1/].

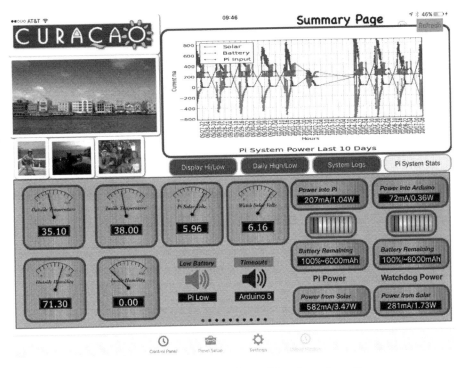

Figure 2-13. *Project Curacao RasPiConnect Control Panel - main page*

Figure 2-14 shows the LightSwarm RasPiConnect control panel running. The control panel shows that there are currently 3 active LightSwarm devices with 125 being the master (with the brightest lights) while the others are slaves. You can send a variety of commands to the swarm, such as resetting a specific swarm device, blinking lights on a swarm device, or resetting the entire swarm.

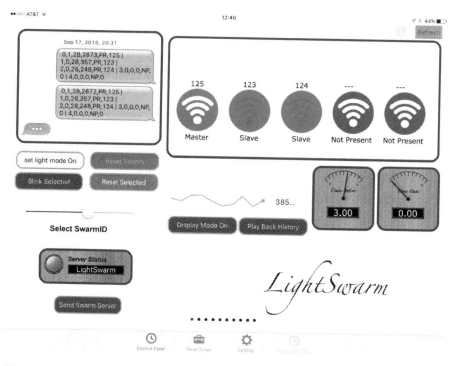

Figure 2-14. LightSwarm RasPiConnect Control Panel

All the software and configuration files for the RasPiConnect server and Apple app are up on the APress download site [The Apress site] and on the github SwitchDoc Labs site [github.com/switchdoclabs/lightswarm_RasPiConnect]

The RasPiConnect server software is pretty straightforward. There is an excellent tutorial for customizing the server software on the MiloCreek web site [www.milocreek.com/wiki].

As an example, Listing 2-20 is the code (located in Local.py) for the Reset Swarm button (as seen on Figure 2-14) and also the code for setting the second from the right meter display in on the LightSwarm control panel.

Listing 2-20. Local.py File for RasPiConnect Code for Reset Swarm Button

```
# Reset Swarm

if (objectServerID == "B-4"):

        #check for validate request
        # validate allows RasPiConnect to verify this object is here
```

```
        if (validate == "YES"):
                outgoingXMLData += Validate.buildValidateResponse("YES")
                outgoingXMLData += BuildResponse.buildFooter()
                return outgoingXMLData

        # normal response requested
        answ = "OK"
        #answ = ""
        if (Config.debug()):
                print "In local B-4"
                print("answ = %s" % answ)

        sendCommandToLightSwarmAndWait("RESETSWARM")

        responseData = "OK"

        outgoingXMLData += BuildResponse.buildResponse(responseData)
        outgoingXMLData += BuildResponse.buildFooter()
        return outgoingXMLData

if (objectServerID == "M-1"):

        #check for validate request
        if (validate == "YES"):
                outgoingXMLData += Validate.buildValidateResponse("YES")
                outgoingXMLData += BuildResponse.buildFooter()

                return outgoingXMLData

        try:
                f = open("/home/pi/LightSwarm/state/LSStatus.txt", "r")
                logString = f.read()
                f.close()
        except:
                logString = ""

        responseData = "%3.2f" % logString.count("PR")
        print "%s = %s" % (objectServerID, responseData)

        outgoingXMLData += BuildResponse.buildResponse(responseData)
        outgoingXMLData += BuildResponse.buildFooter()
        return outgoingXMLData
```

Results

I constructed a LightSwarm consisting of five individual swarm devices. The swarm can be seen in Figure 2-15.

Figure 2-15. *The Light Swarm*

Finally, some results from the devices are shown in Listing 2-21. First of all is the serial debugging output from a LightSwarm device. First the device is initialized, receives an IP address from the WiFi access point (named gracie in this case), and then starts listening and sending packets. The device is swarm device #125 and receives packets from #123 and #122 but remained the master as the CC (Clear Color) of #125 is 2610 while the incoming packets from #123 and #122 had CC values of 310 and 499, respectively, and were both slaves.

Listing 2-21. Results from LightSwarm IOT Device Run on ESP8266

```
--------------------------
LightSwarm
Version 27
--------------------------
 09/03/2015
Compiled at:21:30:47 Sep 16 2015

analogRead(A0)=98
44
Found sensor
LightSwarm Instance: 0
Connecting to gracie
.......................
WiFi connected
IP address:
192.168.1.125
Starting UDP
Local port: 2910
clearColor =0
MySwarmID=0
Color Temp: 2390 K - Lux: 630 - R: 1188 G: 848 B: 440 C: 2610
packetbuffer[1] =0
LIGHT_UPDATE_PACKET received from LightSwarm #123
incomingID 123  assigned #1
LS Packet Recieved from #123 SwarmState:SLAVE CC:310 RC:119 GC:116 BC:69
Version=27
#0/1/27:ME #1/0/27:PR #2/0/0:NP #3/0/0:NP #4/0/0:NP
MasterStatus:MASTER/cc=2610/KS:0.0.0.0
--------
swarmAddress[0] = 125
swarmAddress[1] = 123
swarmAddress[2] = 0
swarmAddress[3] = 0
swarmAddress[4] = 0
--------
Broadcast ToSwarm = 255 Delay = 121ms : Color Temp: 2390 K - Lux: 630 - R:
1188 G: 848 B: 440 C: 2610
packetbuffer[1] =0
LIGHT_UPDATE_PACKET received from LightSwarm #122
incomingID 122  assigned #2
LS Packet Recieved from #122 SwarmState:SLAVE CC:499 RC:231 GC:182 BC:98
Version=27
#0/1/27:ME #1/0/27:PR #2/0/27:PR #3/0/0:NP #4/0/0:NP
MasterStatus:MASTER/cc=2610/KS:0.0.0.0
--------
```

```
swarmAddress[0] = 125
swarmAddress[1] = 123
swarmAddress[2] = 122
swarmAddress[3] = 0
swarmAddress[4] = 0
--------
```

Listing 2-22 is the output from the Raspberry Pi LightSwarm logging software. The first thing the logging software does is send out a "DEFINE_SERVER_LOGGING_PACKET" to tell the swarm devices the IP address (1.168.1.40) of the server so the swarm master can send logging packets directly to the Raspberry Pi, rather than use the already crowded UDP broadcast ports. Finally, we see a packet coming in from SwarmID #111. Number 111 picked up the server address, and since it was the master of the swarm, it started sending in log packets to the Raspberry Pi. Note from the log results, it looks like #111 is a lonely swarm device with no nearby friends.

Listing 2-22. Output from Raspberry Pi LightSwarm Logger

```
--------------
LightSwarm Logger
Version  6
--------------
DEFINE_SERVER_LOGGER_PACKET Sent
lo: 127.0.0.1
eth0: No IP addr
wlan0: 192.168
.1.40
['192.168.1.40']
['192', '168', '1', '40']
DEFINE_SERVER_LOGGER_PACKET Sent
lo: 127.0.0.1
eth0: No IP addr
wlan0: 192.168.1.40
['192.168.1.40']
['192', '168', '1', '40']
Swarm DEFINE_SERVER_LOGGER_PACKET Received
received from addr: ('192.168.1.40', 2910)
incomingID 111
assigned #0
Swarm LOG_TO_SERVER_PACKET Received
Log From SwarmID: 111
Swarm Software Version: 28
StringLength: 80
logString:  0,1,28,1672,PR,111 | 1,0,0,0,NP,0 | 2,0,0,0,NP,0 | 3,0,0,0,NP,0
| 4,0,0,0,NP,0
swarmElement= [' 0', '1', '28', '1672', 'PR', '111 ']
swarmElement= [' 1', '0', '0', '0', 'NP', '0 ']
swarmElement= [' 2', '0', '0', '0', 'NP', '0 ']
```

```
swarmElement= [' 3', '0', '0', '0', 'NP', '0 ']
swarmElement= [' 4', '0', '0', '0', 'NP', '0 ']
swarmElement= [' 3', '0', '0', '0', 'NP', '0 ']
swarmElement= [' 4', '0', '0', '0', 'NP', '0 ']
```

What Else Can You Do with This Architecture?

The LightSwarm architecture is flexible. You can change the sensor, add more sensors, and put in more sophisticated algorithms for swarm behavior. In Chapter 5, we extend this architecture to more complex swarm behavior, actually changing some of the physical environment of the swarm devices.

Conclusion

A good part of the IOT will be the gathering of simple, small amounts of data; some analysis on the data; and the communication of that data to servers for action and further analysis on the Internet. The projects in Chapters 3 and 4 are of more complex IOT devices gathering lots of data, processing it, acting on the data, and communicating summaries to the Internet. The LightSwarm does it differently in that the swarm elements are simple and cooperate without a central controller to determine who has the brightest light and then acting on that information (turning the red LED on).

Swarms of IOT devices can be made inexpensively, can exhibit unexpected complex behavior, and be devilishly difficult to debug.

CHAPTER 3

■ ■ ■

Building a Solar Powered IOT Weather Station

Chapter Goal: Gathering Data and Transmission of Data across the Internet

Topics Covered in This Chapter:

- How to build a solar powered IOT Weather System (Figure 3-1)

- How to design and size the panels and batteries

- How to gather data to analyze your system performance

- How to wire up a Raspberry Pi to a solar power system

- How to safely turn a Raspberry Pi on and off

- How to build the 3D Printed Parts for IOTWeatherPi

- How to connect your Weather Station to the IOT (Tweets, Texts, and CWOP)

© John C. Shovic 2016
J. C. Shovic, *Raspberry Pi IoT Projects*, DOI 10.1007/978-1-4842-1377-3_3

Figure 3-1. *Overall Picture of Station*

Everybody talks about the weather. In this chapter, we are going to talk about the weather in much more detail than just the temperature.

In the previous chapter, we looked at building simple IOT devices that would measure temperature and share that information with a server and other IOT devices. It was a simple application, but still illustrated a number of important concepts. In this chapter, we are building a much more complex and flexible project based on using the Raspberry Pi as part of the IOT device.

The IOTWeatherPi not only gathers thirteen different types of weather data, it also monitors and reports its own state, status, and health.

IOT Characterization of This Project

As I discussed in Chapter 1, the first thing to do to understand an IOT project is to look at our six different aspects of IOT. IOTWeatherPi is a complex product, but Table 3-1 breaks it down into our six components.

Table 3-1. IOTWeatherPi Characterization (CPLPFC)

Aspect	Rating	Comments
Communications	9	WiFi connection to Internet - can do AdHoc mesh-type communication and Bluetooth
Processor Power	7	Raspberry Pi A+ / 256Mb RAM
Local Storage	8	8GB of SD Card
Power Consumption	2	~200mA consumption - Not reasonable for small batteries
Functionality	8	Full Linux-based system. MySQL, etc.
Cost	2	Expensive for many applications. Board is ~$25

Ratings are from 1–10, 1 being the least suitable for IOT and 10 being the most suitable for IOT applications. This gives us a CPLPFC rating of 6. Great for learning, not so good for deployment for most applications.

No doubt about it, the Raspberry Pi is a very flexible and powerful IOT platform. However, the power consumption, cost, and physical size of the device make it more suitable for prototyping or for stand-alone, highly functional IOT units.

How Does This Device Hook Up to the IOT?

With IOTWeatherPi, we have a lot of options. We can hook up to the Internet using the WiFi connector. We can use the Bluetooth to hook up to local devices and we can also use the WiFi in AdHoc mode to make local connections. In this chapter, we will be using the WiFi interface to talk to the wider world of IOT devices.

Data Gathering

The IOTWeatherPi uses thirteen different sensors to detect weather connections. Because I am using a Raspberry Pi and have good storage mechanisms and disk space, I use a MySQL database to store all the weather data for future analysis and download. We also use MatPlotLib to build graphs and use an iOS App called RasPiConnect to display the information across the Internet.

The Project - IOTWeatherPi

WeatherPi is a solar powered Raspberry Pi WiFi connected weather station designed for use in the IOT by the author's company. This is a great system to build and tinker with. All of it is modifiable and all source code is included. Following are the most important functions:

- Senses twenty different environmental values

- Completely Solar Powered

- Has a full database containing history of the environment (MySQL)

- Monitors and reports data on the solar powered system - great for education!

- Self-contained and monitored for brownouts and power issues

- Can be modified remotely

- Download your data to crunch it on your PC

- Can be modified to do SMS (Text) messaging, Twitters, web pages, and more

- Has an iPad-Based Control Panel

- Can connect to the IOT via Twitter, texting, e-mail, and WiFi

This chapter will show you how to build a WiFi Solar Powered Raspberry Pi Weather Station. This project grew out of a number of other projects, including the massive Project Curacao [www.switchdoc.com/project-curacao-introduction-part-1/], a solar powered environmental monitoring system deployed on the Caribbean tropical island of Curacao. Project Curacao was written up in an extensive set of articles in *MagPi* magazine (starting in Issue 18 and continuing through Issue 22).

The IOTWeatherPi Solar Powered Weather Station is an excellent education project. There are many aspects of this project that can be looked at and analyzed for educational purposes:

- How do solar power systems behave? Limitations and advantages.

- Temperature, Wind, and Humidity data analysis.

- Shutting down and starting up small computers on solar power.

- Add your own sensors for UV, dust and pollen count, and light color.

Figure 3-2 shows how IOTWeatherPi is connected to the IOT while Figure 3-3 describes all the major blocks in the project.

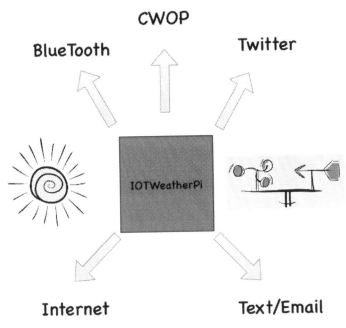

Figure 3-2. *Block Diagram of WeatherPi and the IOT*

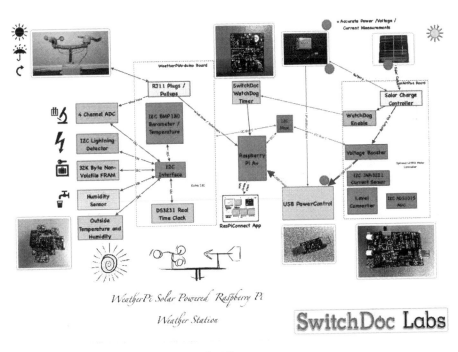

Figure 3-3. *Block Diagram of IOTWeatherPi*

How This All Works

The IOTWeatherPi Block Diagram looks a lot more complicated than it actually is.

The first thing to notice is that the dashed lines are individual boards (WeatherPiArduino and SunAirPlus), which contain a lot of the block diagram; and the second thing is that all of the sensors to the left of the diagram plug into the WeatherPiArduino board, which simplifies the wiring. Don't be intimidated!

The Subsystems

The Power Subsystem of IOTWeatherPi uses a SunAirPlus [www.switchdoc.com/ sunairplus-solar-power-controllerdata-collector/] Solar Power Controller that handles the solar panels, charging of the battery, and then supplies the 5V to the Raspberry Pi and the rest of the system. It also contains sensors that will tell you the current and voltage produced by the Solar Panels and consumed by the batteries and the Raspberry Pi. Gather that Data! Figure 3-4 shows the solar charger board and the battery pack mounted in the top of the enclosure. Figure 3-5 shows the solar cells on the top of outside of the enclosure.

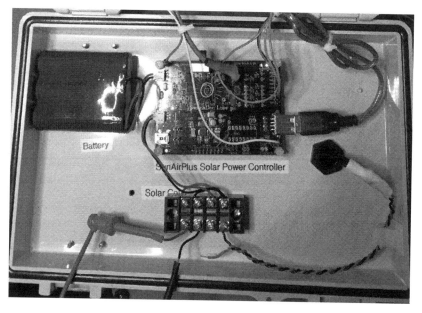

Figure 3-4. *Solar Power Controller*

Figure 3-5. *Solar Cells*

It also contains the hardware watchdog timer and the USB PowerControl that actually shuts off the power to the Raspberry Pi during a brownout event (after the Pi shuts gracefully down under software control).

The Sensor Subsystem of IOTWeatherPi uses a WeatherPiArduino [www.switchdoc. com/weatherpiarduino-bare-board/] as the base unit and then plugs in a bunch of optional sensors such as wind speed / direction / rain, lightning detection (how cool is that!), inside and outside temperature, and humidity. Figure 3-6 pictures the wind and rain sensors.

Figure 3-6. *Wind / Rain Sensors*

The *Software Subsystem* of IOTWeatherPi runs in Python on the Raspberry Pi. It collects the data, stores in in a MySQL database, builds graphs, and does housekeeping and power monitoring.

The IOTWeatherPi Sensor Suite senses the following environmental values:

- Wind Speed

- Wind Direction

- Rain

- Outside Temperature

- Outside Humidity

- Lightning Detection

- Barometric Pressure (and Altitude)

- Inside Box Temperature

- Inside Box Humidity

You can add more to the I2C bus and Analog to Digital Converter such as UV, dust counts, light color (sensing some types of pollution), and more! It's a great platform for expansion.

The sensor suite is built on the WeatherPiArduino (shown in Figure 3-7) board but there are several similar boards out there on the market.

Figure 3-7. WeatherPiArduino

The I2C Bus

WeatherPi makes extensive use of the I2C bus on the Raspberry Pi.

At SwitchDoc Labs, we love data. And we love I2C devices. We like to gather the data using lots of I2C devices on our computers and projects. Project Curacao has a total of twelve, IOTWeatherPi has eleven devices, and SunRover (a solar powered IOT connected robot under development at SwitchDoc) will have over twenty and will require one I2C bus just for controlling the motors. We are always running into conflicts with addressing on the I2C device. Since there are no standards, sometimes multiple devices will have the same address, such as 0x70; and you are just out of luck in running both of them on the same I2C bus without a lot of jimmy rigging. Figure 3-8 shows the I2C Mux wired into the project.

Figure 3-8. *I2CMux in IOTWeatherPi*

To get around this addressing problem (and our conflict with an INA3221 and the Inside Humidity Sensor) we added an I2C Bus Multiplexer to the design, which allows us to have many more I2C devices on the bus, regardless of addressing conflicts. Table 3-2 provides a list of I2C devices in IOTWeatherPi.

Table 3-2. *I2C Addresses in IOTWeatherPi*

Device	I2C Address
BMP180 or BMP280 Barometric Pressure	0x77
Real Time Clock DS3231	0x68
ATC EEPROM	0x56
ADS1015 Analog to Digital Converter	0x49
FRAM Non-volatile storage	0x50
ADS1015 on SunAirPlus	0x48
INA3221 3 Channel Voltage/Current Monitor on SunAirPlus	0x40
HTU21D-F Humidity Sensor	0x40
Embedded Adventures Lightning Detector	0x03
AM2315 Outdoor Temp/Humidity	0x5C
I2C 4 Channel I2C Bus Mux	0x73

Following is what the I2C bus looks like on the Raspberry Pi. There are four independent buses shown for the I2C bus, but note that IOTWeatherPi only uses Bus 0 and Bus 1. Figure 3-9 shows a fully populated WeatherPiArduino board.

```
Test SDL_Pi_TCA9545 Version 1.0 - SwitchDoc Labs

Sample uses 0x73
Program Started at:2015-05-10 20:00:56

-----------BUS 0-------------------
tca9545 control register B3-B0 = 0x1
ignore Interrupts if INT3' - INT0' not connected
tca9545 control register Interrupts = 0xc
     0  1  2  3  4  5  6  7  8  9  a  b  c  d  e  f
00:          03 -- -- -- -- -- -- -- -- -- -- -- --
10: -- -- -- -- -- -- -- -- -- -- -- -- -- -- -- --
20: -- -- -- -- -- -- -- -- -- -- -- -- -- -- -- --
30: -- -- -- -- -- -- -- -- -- -- -- -- -- -- -- --
40: 40 -- -- -- -- -- -- -- -- 49 -- -- -- -- -- --
50: 50 -- -- -- -- -- 56 -- -- -- -- -- -- -- -- --
60: -- -- -- -- -- -- -- -- 68 -- -- -- -- -- -- --
70: -- -- -- 73 -- -- -- 77

-----------------------------------
```

```
-----------BUS 1-------------------
tca9545 control register B3-B0 = 0x2
ignore Interrupts if INT3' - INT0' not connected
tca9545 control register Interrupts = 0xe
     0  1  2  3  4  5  6  7  8  9  a  b  c  d  e  f
00:          -- -- -- -- -- -- -- -- -- -- -- -- --
10: -- -- -- -- -- -- -- -- -- -- -- -- -- -- -- --
20: -- -- -- -- -- -- -- -- -- -- -- -- -- -- -- --
30: -- -- -- -- -- -- -- -- -- -- -- -- -- -- -- --
40: 40 -- -- -- -- -- -- -- 48 -- -- -- -- -- -- --
50: -- -- -- -- -- -- -- -- -- -- -- -- -- -- -- --
60: -- -- -- -- -- -- -- -- -- -- -- -- -- -- -- --
70: -- -- -- 73 -- -- -- --


-----------------------------------


-----------BUS 2-------------------
tca9545 control register B3-B0 = 0x4
ignore Interrupts if INT3' - INT0' not connected
tca9545 control register Interrupts = 0xc
     0  1  2  3  4  5  6  7  8  9  a  b  c  d  e  f
00:          -- -- -- -- -- -- -- -- -- -- -- -- --
10: -- -- -- -- -- -- -- -- -- -- -- -- -- -- -- --
20: -- -- -- -- -- -- -- -- -- -- -- -- -- -- -- --
30: -- -- -- -- -- -- -- -- -- -- -- -- -- -- -- --
40: -- -- -- -- -- -- -- -- -- -- -- -- -- -- -- --
50: -- -- -- -- -- -- -- -- -- -- -- -- -- -- -- --
60: -- -- -- -- -- -- -- -- -- -- -- -- -- -- -- --
70: -- -- -- 73 -- -- -- --


-----------------------------------


-----------BUS 3-------------------
tca9545 control register B3-B0 = 0x8
ignore Interrupts if INT3' - INT0' not connected
tca9545 control register Interrupts = 0xc
     0  1  2  3  4  5  6  7  8  9  a  b  c  d  e  f
00:          -- -- -- -- -- -- -- -- -- -- -- -- --
10: -- -- -- -- -- -- -- -- -- -- -- -- -- -- -- --
20: -- -- -- -- -- -- -- -- -- -- -- -- -- -- -- --
30: -- -- -- -- -- -- -- -- -- -- -- -- -- -- -- --
40: -- -- -- -- -- -- -- -- -- -- -- -- -- -- -- --
50: -- -- -- -- -- -- -- -- -- -- -- -- -- -- -- --
60: -- -- -- -- -- -- -- -- -- -- -- -- -- -- -- --
70: -- -- -- 73 -- -- -- --


-----------------------------------
```

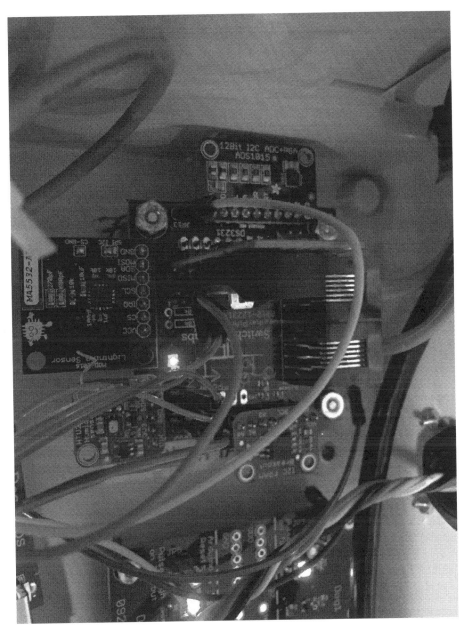

Figure 3-9. *WeatherPiArduino Fully Loaded with Sensors*

Sizing Your Solar Power System

One of the first things that comes up in a solar powered design is how to design the power system. The three main questions to be asked and answered are the following:

1. How much power do I need?

2. How many solar panels do I need?

3. What size battery do I need?

The first thing you need to do when designing a solar powered system is to determine the power requirements for your solar powered design. Our criteria are that we want the IOTWeatherPi Raspberry Pi Model A to run all day and at least three hours before sunrise and three hours after sunset. Our goals and budget influence our hardware choices, so they are not totally independent. Figure 3-10 shows the solar panels with the AM2315 outside temperature sensor on the side of the enclosure.

Figure 3-10. Solar Power Panels on IOTWeatherPi

Table 3-3 contains estimated power consumption for models of the Raspberry Pi, including a Wireless USB dongle. We are assuming in each of these that you turn the HDMI port off, which saves ~20mA.

Table 3-3. Estimated Power Consumption for Raspberry Pi Models

	Model A	Model A+	Model B	Model B+	Model Pi2 B
Current (mA)	260(200)	195(135)	480(420)	290(230)	304(240)
Power (W)	1.3(1.0)	0.975 (0.675)	2.4 (2.1)	1.45 (1.15)	1.52 (1.2)
Source	Measured	Measured	Measured	Measured	Measured

All of the above measurements include about 60mA for the USB WiFi Dongle. Parenthetical numbers are without the 60mA.

Based on the above, first I will lay out my assumptions for our Raspberry Pi Model A+-based design. The LiPo batteries chosen will store 6600mAh. Why choose the Model A+? It's the lowest current consuming Raspberry Pi.

What is mAh (milli Amp hours)? A 6600mAh means you can take 100mA for 66 hours, theoretically. In actuality, you will not be able to get more than about 80% on average depending on your battery. How fast you discharge them also makes a big difference. The slower the discharge rate, the more mAh you can get out of the battery. For comparison, an AA battery will hold about 1000mAh[en.wikipedia.org/wiki/AA_battery] and a D battery will hold about 10000mAh[en.wikipedia.org/wiki/AA_battery].

In a system like this, it is best to charge your LiPo batteries completely and then hook up the computer and see how long it takes to discharge the battery and die. We did this test on the IOTWeatherPi system. The results are here on switchdoc.com [www.switchdoc.com/?p=1926].

Assumptions:

- Two Voltaic 3.4W 6V/530ma Solar Cells (total of 6.8W)

    - 8 Hours of Sun running the cells at least at 70% of max Delivery of current to Raspberry Pi at 85% efficiency (you lose power in the charging and boosting circuitry)

- Raspberry Pi Model A+ takes 195mA on average (with the Wireless USB Dongle)

    - Raspberry Pi Model A+ running 24 hours per day

    - 6600mAh LiPo Batteries

Given these we can calculate total Raspberry Pi Model A runtime during a typical day:

```
PiRunTime = (8 Hours * 70% * 1060mA) *85% / (195mA) = 25 hours
```

Our goal was for 24 hours, so it looks like our system will work. So 16 Hours of running the Raspberry Pi Model A+ on batteries alone will take (195mA/85%)*16 Hours = 3670mAh, which is comfortably less than our 6600mAh batteries can store. The WIFI dongle added about 60mA on average. It was enabled the entire time the Raspberry Pi was on. No effort was made to minimize the power consumed by the WiFi dongle. Your results will depend on what other loads you are driving, such as other USB devices, GPIO loads, I2C devices, etc.

Note that during the day, on average, we are putting into the battery about 6000mAh.

This also means a larger battery than 6600mAh will not make much difference to this system.

So, on a bright sunny day, we should be able to run 24 hours a day. Looking at the results from IOTWeatherPi being out in the sun for a week, this seems to be correct. However, it will be cloudy and rainy and your system will run out of power. The next most-important part of the design is how to handle brownouts! See the section below about how to hand this nasty little problem.

The four most important parts of verifying your Solar Power Design:

- Gather real data;

- Gather more real data;

- Gather still more real data;

- Look at your data and what it is telling you about the real system. Rinse and Repeat.

Power Up and Power Down

The power system in Weather Pi consists of four parts:

- Two Solar Panels

- One 6600Ah LiPo Battery

- SunAirPlus Solar Power Controller, Pi Power Supply; and Data Gathering system

- USB PowerControl board for Pi Power Control

We are using 2 3.4W Solar Panels from Voltaic Systems. These are high-quality panels that we have used in previous projects and last a long time even in the tropical sun. The picture above is of the same panels on Project Curacao after six months in the sun. Those are clouds reflected on the panels, not dirt. The panels are perfect.

We selected a 6600mAh battery from Adafruit for this design. See the "Sizing your Solar System" step below.

We are using a SunAirPlus Solar Power Controller in this design. In Figure 3-11 you can see how the solar power control is placed in the enclosure, above the Raspberry Pi.

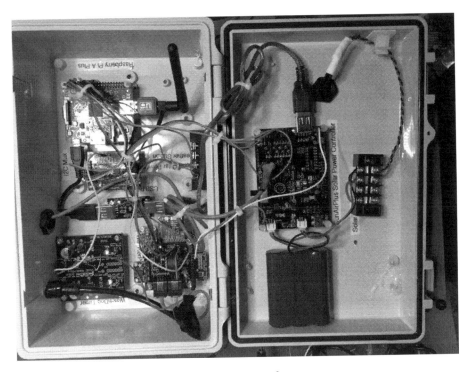

Figure 3-11. *Solar Power Controller in Lower Part of Box*

SunAirPlus includes an I2C INA3221[www.switchdoc.com/2015/03/sunairplus-solar-power-ina3221-python-raspberry-pi-library-released/] 3 Channel Current / Voltage Monitor and a I2C 4 channel 12 bit Analog to Digital Converter (ADS1015). The INA3221 allows you to monitor all of the major currents and voltages in the system (Battery / Solar Panels / Load - Computer). You can tell what your solar power project is doing in real time.

Following are some results from the SunAirPlus board using the onboard INA3221. You can see that the battery is almost fully charged, and the solar cell voltage (actually a variable power supply on the test bench) is 5.19V and it is supplying 735mA.

```
Test SDL_Pi_INA3221 Version 1.0 - SwitchDoc Labs

Sample uses 0x40 and SunAirPlus board INA3221
Will work with the INA3221 SwitchDoc Labs Breakout Board

-----------------------------
LIPO_Battery Bus Voltage: 4.15 V
LIPO_Battery Shunt Voltage: -9.12 mV
LIPO_Battery Load Voltage:  4.14 V
LIPO_Battery Current 1:  91.20 mA
```

```
Solar Cell Bus Voltage 2:   5.19 V
Solar Cell Shunt Voltage 2: -73.52 mV
Solar Cell Load Voltage 2:  5.12 V
Solar Cell Current 2:   735.20 mA


Output Bus Voltage 3:   4.88 V
Output Shunt Voltage 3: 48.68 mV
Output Load Voltage 3:   4.93 V
Output Current 3:   486.80 mA
```

You can use this board to power your projects and add a servo or stepper motor to allow it to track the sun using photoresistors to generate even more power.

The USB PowerController Board is basically a controlled Solid State Relay to turn the power on and off to the Raspberry Pi. This board sits between the Solar Power Controller (SunAirPlus) and a Raspberry Pi Model A+. The input to the board was designed to come directly from a LiPo battery so the computer won't be turned on until the LiPo battery was charged up above ~ 3.8V. A hysteresis circuit is provided so the board won't turn on and then turn immediately off because the power supply is yanked down when the computer turns on (immediately putting a load on the battery). This really happens!!!! You kill Raspberry Pi SD Cards this way.

The Brownout Problem

In this important step, we are going to discuss the problem of powering down and up your Raspberry Pi. In Solar Powered systems, this is called the "Brownout Problem." We will be showing how to use a simple device, the USB Power Control [www.switchdoc.com/usb-powercontrol-board/], from SwitchDoc Labs to solve this problem.

One of the most important issues in designing a Raspberry Pi Solar Power System is turning on and off. The "Brownout Problem" is a real issue. Why worry? If you have a long string of cloudy days, you may run your battery down. You can compensate for this in your design by adding more panels and more batteries, but that can get really expensive and your system might still run out of power, just a lot less frequently.

Shutting Off the Pi

Shutting a Raspberry Pi off is pretty easy. When the battery voltage falls below some value, you just do a "sudo shutdown -h now" and your Raspberry Pi will shut down cleanly. After doing the test talked about here [www.switchdoc.com/?p=1926], we chose 3.5V as the voltage to shut down the Raspberry Pi. Figure 3-12 shows the graph of the data after implementing these values.

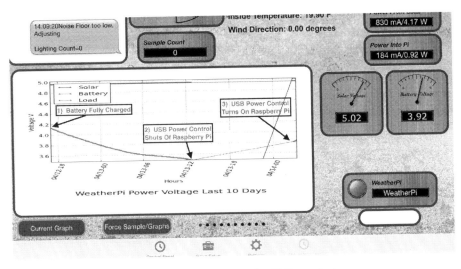

Figure 3-12. *Testing the Behavior of the IOTWeatherPi Power System*

Note that in most solar power systems, you need to monitor the battery voltage and not the 5V power supply because with most modern voltage booster systems, the circuitry will work very hard to keep the 5V going and then just give up crashing to a much lower voltage when it runs out of power.

That means your computer would have little or no warning when the voltage is about to drop. By monitoring the battery voltage, you can tell when the battery is getting low enough and then shut down your computer safely. For LiPo batteries, this will be when your voltage gets down to about 3.5V or so. This can all be monitored with the SunAirPlus solar charge controller that we are using in IOTWeatherPi.

Starting the Pi

Enough about shutting down the computer. What about starting it up?

The Issue

You can't just let the controller power up the computer. The problem is that the supply voltage will move up and down until there is enough charge in the battery to fully supply the computer. When the computer turns on (connecting a full load), you will pull the battery down hard enough to brown out the computer causing the Raspberry Pi to crash. This constant rebooting cycle can corrupt and ruin your SD card and cause your computer to never boot at all, even when the power is restored. We had this VERY thing happen to us 3500 miles away with Project Curacao[www.switchdoc.com/2015/02/solar-power-project-curacao-update/]. Arduinos are more tolerant of this, but Raspberry Pi's do not like an ill-behaved power supply. You just can't be sure of what state the computer will power up at without a good power supply.

This issue can be handled in a number of ways. The first is to use another computer (like an Arduino made to be very reliable by using a WatchDog - see the Reliable Computer series on switchdoc.com [www.switchdoc.com/2014/11/reliable-projects-watchdog-timers-raspberry-pi-arduinos/)]to disconnect the Raspberry Pi's power through a latching relay or MOSFET when there isn't enough power. Project Curacao (www.switchdoc.com/project-curacao-introduction-part-1/) used this approach.

We didn't want to add an additional computer to IOTWeatherPi, so we chose a second solution.

Power Your Pi Up and Down with the USB Power Control

A second (and cheaper!) way of handling the brownout and power-up problem is to use a dedicated power controller that will shut the power off to the Raspberry Pi and restore the power when the battery voltage is high enough to avoid ratcheting the supply voltage up and down because of the load of the Raspberry Pi. This is called Hysteresis. We have designed a board to do just this (called the USB PowerController[www.switchdoc.com/usb-powercontrol-board/]) that will plug between the USB coming out of the SunAir Solar Power Controller and the Raspberry Pi as in Figure 3-13.

Figure 3-13. *USB PowerControl*

The USB Power Controller Board

The USB PowerControl board is a USB to USB solid state relay.

Anything you can plug into a USB port can be controlled with USB PowerControl. It's easy to hook up. You connect a control line (a GPIO line or the output of a LiPo battery) to the LIPOBATIN line on the USB Power Control device and if the line is LOW (< ~3.3V) the USB Port is off. If it is HIGH (above 3.8V) the USB Port is turned on and you have 5V of power to the USB plug.

There is a hysteresis circuit so the board won't turn on and then turn immediately off because the power supply is yanked down when the computer turns on (putting a load on the battery).

There is little software for this device. You connect it directly to your LiPo battery for automatic control! The only software used detects the battery voltage and decides when to shut down the computer. The USB Power Control takes care of shutting the power to the Raspberry Pi when the battery voltage gets low enough. Note that a shutdown Raspberry Pi still draws current (according to one quick measurement, about 100mA). Figure 3-14 shows how you integrate the USB PowerControl into a system.

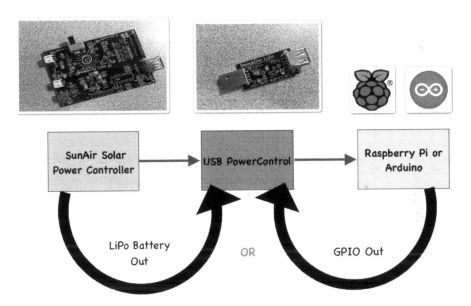

Figure 3-14. *Controlling the Raspberry Pi Power*

One More Scenario

One last point. After thinking about the power down sequence, we came up with one more scenario. What if:

1. The battery voltage reaches 3.5V and the Raspberry Pi is shut down.

2. The USB PowerController will turn the power off when the battery reaches about 3.4V.

However, what if the sun comes up at this time and the battery starts charging again? Then the USB PowerController will never reach about 3.4V and will never turn off. And the Pi will never reboot. Not a good scenario!

We fixed this by adding a hardware watchdog timer. For a tutorial on hardware watchdog timers, read the SwitchDoc series starting here [www.switchdoc.com/2014/11/reliable-projects-watchdog-timers-raspberry-pi-arduinos/]. A picture of the WatchDog Timer is given in Figure 3-15.

Figure 3-15. WatchDog Timer

We used a Dual WatchDog Timer Board [www.switchdoc.com/dual-watchdog-timer/] to fix this problem. We set the RaspberryPi python to "pat the dog" (preventing the watchdog timer from triggering) every 10 seconds. The timer is set to trigger after about 200 seconds if it isn't patted. The timer is connected to pull the "COut" (TP3) point down to ground on the USB PowerController, which shuts off the Raspberry Pi. Because of the hysteresis circuit on the USB PowerController, the Raspberry Pi will stay off until the battery voltage reaches ~3.9V and then the Pi will reboot. Now the above scenario will never happen. By the way, there is no real way of using the internal Pi Watchdog to do this. You don't want to reboot the Pi; you want to shut off the power in this scenario.

■ **SwitchDoc Tip**   Building wiring cables is always a pain. You want all the wires to be together and you want them to be compact and nice looking. One great way of doing this is to cut the hook-up wires to the same length and then braid them together by using an electric drill. You insert the wires and then spin the drill slowly while running your fingers slowly up the wires. Good-looking cables every time! Figure 3-16 shows the result. Nice-looking cables.

Figure 3-16. Braided Cables with Drill

What Do You Need to Build This Project?

No project is complete without a parts list. These are suggestions. There are many options for a number of these boards. If you substitute, make sure you check for compatibility. Figure 3-17 shows all of the parts.

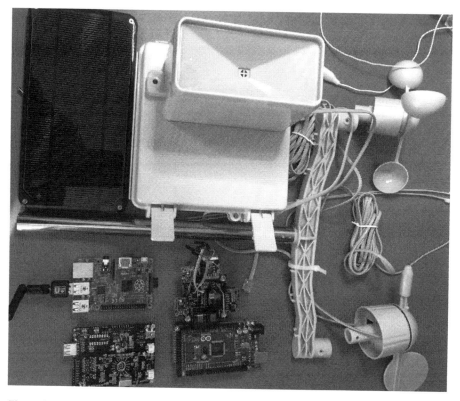

Figure 3-17. *IOTWeatherPi Parts*

- WeatherRack Weather Sensors [www.switchdoc.com/weatherrack-weather-sensors/]

- BUD NEMA Box from amazon.com [www.amazon.com/gp/product/B005T57WYI/r&tag=wwwswitchdoo5-20]

- VoltaicSystems Solar Panel(s) - 2 panels [www.voltaicsystems.com/3-5-watt-panel]

- Raspberry Pi A+, Raspberry Pi 2, Raspberry Pi 3 (the lower the power the better)

- Raspberry Pi Compatible WiFi USB Dongle

- SunAirPlus Solar Power Controller [`www.switchdoc.com/sunairplus-solar-power-controllerdata-collector/`]

- USB PowerControl [`www.switchdoc.com/usb-powercontrol-board/`]

- Grove 4 Channel I2C Mux Breakout Board w/Status LEDs [`www.switchdoc.com/grove-i2c-4-channel-mux-board-wstatus-leds/`]

- SwitchDoc Labs Dual WatchDog Timer [`www.switchdoc.com/dual-watchdog-timer/`]

- WeatherPiArduino Weather Board [`www.switchdoc.com/weatherboard/`]

- Embedded Adventures I2C Lightning Detector MOD-1016 board [`www.embeddedadventures.com/as3935_lightning_sensor_module_mod-1016.html`]

- DS3231 RTC With EEPROM [`www.switchdoc.com/ds3231-real-time-clock-module/`]

- AM2315 Outdoor Temperature and Humidity Sensor [`www.switchdoc.com/am2315-encased-i2c-temperature-and-humidity-sensor/`]

- BMP180 Barometer and Temperature Sensor [`www.switchdoc.com/wp-content/uploads/2015/01/BST-BMP180-DS000-09.pdf`]

- Adafruit HTU21D-F Temperature/Humidity breakout board

- Adafruit 32KB FRAM I2C breakout board

- Adafruit ADS1015 4 Channel A/D I2C board

- Adafruit PKCELL Lithium Ion Battery Pack - 3.7V 6600mAh

- Waterproof 8 Pin Plug from amazon.com [`www.amazon.com/gp/product/B00HG9V00S/&tag=wwwswitchdo05-20`]

- 2 Dual Row 4 Position Covered Screw Terminal Block Strip from amazon.com [`www.amazon.com/gp/product/B00SUXK2ZM/&tag=wwwswitchdocc-20`]

- RasPiConnect Control Panel [`www.milocreek.com/`]

Connecting and Testing the Hardware

As with most projects, we tend to "breadboard" the circuitry before we put it into the enclosure. With IOTWeatherPi, we spread out the parts, wired them up, made sure each of the major paths worked (and of course, took the obligatory nighttime geek shot), and then started placing them in the box, attaching them with screws and posts through the plastic. Figure 3-18 shows the wired project at night before placing it in the enclosure.

Figure 3-18. *IOTWeatherPi at Night*

Putting the IOTWeatherPi into the BUD Industries box was pretty straight forward. We chose to put the solar power part of the circuit on top and the Raspberry Pi and the IOTWeatherPiArduino Sensor array in the box bottom. The parts were all placed and then all the screw holes and outside screws were sealed with silicon caulking.

We used Gland Connectors to run the wires in and out of the box. Then we sealed the Gland Connectors. The Gland Connectors aren't necessarily waterproof, but they make things tighter and provide a good strain relief. We then used a waterproof disconnectable plug to tie into the WeatherRack weather instruments. You can see these connections in Figure 3-19.

Figure 3-19. IOTWeatherPi Connections

In building the IOTWeatherPi Solar Powered Weather Station, we saw a couple of parts that we decided would be good to 3D Print. In the twelve months since we bought our SwitchDoc Labs MakerBot Replicator [makerbot.com/], wc have totally changed the way we build special parts for prototyping. And with the latest extruder and firmware updates, the MakerBot rocks! I have done ten long prints with no problem. It used to be Xacto knives and foam, wood and glue, but now we just build new parts when we need them. Figure 3-20 shows the completed 3D Printed parts. The three parts we have used 3D Printing for are the following:

- Bracket with Hinges to connect solar panel panels to weather station box (adjustable for latitude);

- Opposite hinge on which to hang solar power panels (the tabs on the side of the rectangle are just to make sure the bracket is flat!);

- Sun Cover for AM2315 Temperature and Humidity Sensor - we killed the Humidity sensor by not covering the AM2315 in Project Curacao [www.switchdoc.com/project-curacao-environmental-subsystem-part-4/].

Figure 3-20. 3D Printed Parts

The OpenSCAD files for building these parts are located at www.switchdoc.com/wp-content/uploads/2015/04/WeatherPi3D-041115.zip.

The Full Wiring List

Table 3-4 provides the complete wiring list for IOTWeatherPi. As you wire it, check off each wire for accuracy.

Key:

> Raspberry Pi A+: **PiA+**
>
> Grove I2C Bus Mux: **GI2CM**
>
> Dual WatchDog Timer Board: **WDT**
>
> WeatherPiArduino: **WPA**
>
> USB Power Control: **USBPC**
>
> SunAirPlus: **SAP**

Table 3-4. *IOTWeatherPi Wiring List*

Raspberry Pi A+ (PiA+)

GPIO Header

From	*To*	*Description*
PiA+ GPIO/Pin 1: 3.3V	IGI2CM JP1/Pin 3:VCC	Power for I2C Mux Board - Computer Interface
PiA+ GPIO/Pin 2: 5.0V	WDT JP1/Pin 1:VDD	Power for Dual WatchDog Timer Board
PiA+ GPIO/Pin 3: SDA	GI2CM JP1/Pin2:SDA	SDA for I2C Mux Board - Computer Interface
PiA+ GPIO/Pin 5: SCL	GI2CM JP1/Pin1:SCL	SCL for I2C Mux Board - Computer Interface
PiA+ GPIO/Pin 6: GND	GI2CM JP1/Pin4:GND	GND for I2C Mux Board - Computer Interface
PiA+ GPIO/Pin 11 GPIO 17	WDT JP2/Pin1:DOG1_ TRIGGER	Trigger Input for WatchDog 1 Timer (Pat the Dog)
PiA+ GPIO/Pin 12: GPIO 18	WPA JP13/Pin1: LD-IRQ	Interrupt Request from the AS3935 on Lightning Detector Board
PiA+ GPIO/Pin 16: GPIO 23	WPA JP2/ Pin3:Anemometer	Anemometer Output from WeatherRack - Interrupt
PiA+ GPIO/Pin 17: 3.3V	VCC Screw Connector	To provide more 3.3V Connections
PiA+ GPIO/Pin 18: GPIO 24	WPA JP2/Pin 2:Rain Bucket	Rain Bucket Output from WeatherRack - Interrupt
PiA+ GPIO/Pin 22: GPIO 25	SAP JP13/Pin8: EXTGP0	GP0 on SunAir Board - Yellow LED display

Grove I2C Mux Board (GI2CM)

From	*To*	*Description*
JP1 - Computer		
GI2CM JP1/Pin 2:SDA	PiA+ GPIO/Pin 3:SDA	SDA to I2C Mux Board - Computer Interface
GI2CM JP1/Pin 1: SCL	PiA+ GPIO/Pin 5:SDA	SCL to I2C Mux Board - Computer Interface
GI2CM JP1/Pin 4: GND	PiA+ GPIO/Pin 6:GND	GND for I2C Mux Board - Computer Interface

(*continued*)

Table 3-4. (*continued*)

Raspberry Pi A+ (PiA+)		
GI2CM JP1/Pin 3: VCC	PiA+ GPIO/Pin 1: 3.3V	Power for I2C Mux Board - Computer Interface
JP2 - I2C Bus 0	WeatherPiArduino I2C Bus	
GI2CM JP2/Pin 3: VDU0	WPA JP1/Pin 2: VDD	3.3V from WPA Board
GI2CM JP2/Pin 2: GND	WPA JP1/Pin 1: GND	GND for WPA Board
GI2CM JP2/Pin 5: SC0	WPA JP4/Pin 1: SCL	SCL for WPA Board
GI2CM JP2/Pin 4: SD0	WPA JP4/Pin 2: SDA	SDA for WPA Board
JP3 - I2C Bus 1	SunAirPlus I2C Bus	
GI2CM JP3/Pin 3: VDU1	SPA JP23/Pin 3: VDD	5.0V for Bus 1 for I2C Mux
GI2CM JP3/Pin 2: GND	SAP JP13/Pin 4: GND	GND for SAP Board
GI2CM JP3/Pin 5: SC1	SAP JP13/Pin 1: EXTSCL	SCL for SAP Board
GI2CM JP3/Pin 4: SD1	SAP JP13/Pin 2: EXTSDA	SDA for SAP Board
JP4 - I2C Bus 3	Auxiliary GND for WDT Board	GND for WDT Board
GI2CM JP4/Pin2: GND	WDT JP1/Pin 1:GND	GND for WDT Board
Dual WatchDog Timer Board (WDT)		
From	*To*	*Description*
JP1		
WDT JP1/Pin 1: VDD	PiA+ GPIO/Pin 2:VDD (5.0V)	
WDT JP1/Pin 2: GND	GI2CM JP4/Pin 2:GND	GND for WDT Board
JP2		
WDT JP2/Pin 1: DOG1_ TRIGGER	PiA+ GPIO/Pin 11:GPIO 17	WDT Trigger from Raspberry Pi
JP3		
WDT JP3/Pin 1: DOG1_ ARDUINORESET	USBPC: TP3 - COUT	Solder Wire to TP3 - COUT on USB PowerControl

(*continued*)

Table 3-4. (*continued*)

Raspberry Pi A+ (PiA+)		

WeatherPiArduino (WPA)

From	*To*	*Description*
JP1		
WPA JP1/Pin 1: GND	GI2CMux JP2/Pin 2: GND	GND for WPA Board from I2CMux
WPA JP1/Pin 2: 3V3	GI2CMux JP2/Pin 3: VDU0	3.3V for I2C Bus 0 from WPA
JP2		
WPA JP2/Pin 2: Rain Bucket	PiA+ GPIO/Pin 18: GPIO 24	Rain Bucket Output from WeatherRack - Interrupt
WPA JP2/Pin 3: Anemometer	PiA+ GPIO/Pin 16: GPIO 23	Anemometer Output from WeatherRack - Interrupt
JP4		
WPA JP4/Pin 1: SCL	GI2CMux JP4/Pin 5: SCL	SCL from I2C Mux Board
WPA JP4/Pin 2: SDA	GI2CMux JP4/Pin 4: SDA	SDA from I2C Mux Board
WPA JP4/Pin 3: 3V3	VCC Screw Connector	3.3V From Pi/Screw Connector
JP13		
WPA JP13/Pin 1: LD-IRQ	PiA+ GPIO/Pin 12: GPIO 18	Interrupt Request from the AS3935 on Lightning Detector Board

USB Power Control (USBPC)

From	*To*	*Description*
USBIN: USB Connector from SAP	USB A OUT on SAP	
USBOUT: USB Connector to PiA+	USB Power Input on PiA+	
JP1		
USBOUT JP1/Pin 1: LIPOBATIN	SAP JP4/Pin1: LiPo Battery Out	SAP Plus of LiPo Battery Out to USB PowerControl
TP3 - COUT:	WDT JP3/Pin 1: DOG1_ ARDUINORESET	Shuts USB Power Control down if Raspberry Pi has been shut down and LIPOBATIN < ~3.9V

(*continued*)

Table 3-4. (*continued*)

Raspberry Pi A+ (PiA+)		
SunAirPlus (SAP)		
From	*To*	*Description*
USB A Out:	USBIN on USBPC	
J5 Battery:	To LiPo Battery Pack	
J6 Solar:	To Solar Panels	
JP4		
SAP JP4/Pin 1:	USBPC: JP1/Pin1 LIPOBATIN	SAP Plus of LiPo Battery Out to USB PowerControl
JP10		
SAP JP10/Pin 1: SCL	SCL (5.0V)	Connected to Outdoor Temp/Hum AM2315 Sensor - works better on 5.0V I2C Bus
SAP JP10/Pin 2: SDA	SDA (5.0V)	Connected to Outdoor Temp/Hum AM2315 Sensor - works better on 5.0V I2C Bus
SAP JP10/Pin 3: VDD5	VDD5	Connected to Outdoor Temp/Hum AM2315 Sensor - works better on 5.0V I2C Bus
SAP JP10/Pin 4: GND	GND	Connected to Outdoor Temp/Hum AM2315 Sensor - works better on 5.0V I2C Bus
JP13		
SAP JP13/Pin 1: EXTSCL	GI2CMux JP3/Pin 5: SC1	
SAP JP13/Pin 2: EXTSDA	GI2CMux JP3/Pin 4: SD1	
SAP JP13/Pin 3: VDD	SPA JP23/Pin2: VDD5	5V I2C Interface from SAP
SAP JP13/Pin 4: GND	GI2CMux JP3/Pin 2: GND	GND form I2CMux Board
SAP JP13/Pin 8: EXTGP0	PiA+ GPIO/Pin 22: GPIO 25	Line from Raspberry Pi to flash SAP Yellow LED on GP0
JP23		
SAP JP23/Pin 2: VDD5	SAP JP13/Pin 3: VDD	5.0V for SAP I2C Bus to I2CMux
SAP JP23/Pin 3: VDD5	GI2CMux JP3/Pin 3: VDU1	5.0V for I2CMux I2C Bus1

The Software

A big part of the IOTWeatherPi Project is the software. All of the Python software for this project is up on github at the switchdoclabs section [https://github.com/switchdoclabs/WeatherPi]. I also included all of the various libraries for the I2C devices we are using.

Non-Normal Requirements for your Pi

You will need to add the following software and libraries to your Raspberry Pi:

- MySQL. There are lots of tutorials on the Internet for installing MySQL. Here is the one we used [raspberrywebserver.com/sql-databases/using-mysql-on-a-raspberry-pi.html]. The structure of the WeatherPi MySQL database in mysqldump format is located on github [https://github.com/switchdoclabs/WeatherPiSQL]. You can use this file to build the MySQL database for the IOTWeatherPi Project.

- MatPlotLib. This is the graphing subsystem with a great interface to Python. It is a bit more complex to install, so I wrote a tutorial on how to install it on SwitchDoc.com[www.switchdoc.com/2014/01/matplotlib-raspberry-pi-mysql-and-project-curacao/]. Note that the installation takes a long time, about eight hours on a Raspberry Pi (mostly unattended).

The IOTWeatherPi Python Software

The IOTWeatherPi software is pretty simple. The application was much less complex than the Project Curacao software [,www.switchdoc.com/project-curacao-software-system-part-6/] so I decided not use the apscheduler package and decided just to use a simple loop with an "every 15 seconds" type of control. Here is the main loop:

```
secondCount = 1
while True:

        # process Interrupts from Lightning

        if (as3935Interrupt == True):
                process_as3935_interrupt()

        # process commands from RasPiConnect
        print "-------------------------------------- "

        processCommand()
```

```
if ((secondCount % 10) == 0):
        # print every 10 seconds
        sampleAndDisplay()
        patTheDog()        # reset the WatchDog Timer
        blinkSunAirLED2X(2)

# every 5 minutes, push data to mysql and check for shutdown

if ((secondCount % (5*60)) == 0):
        # print every 300 seconds
        sampleWeather()
        sampleSunAirPlus()
        writeWeatherRecord()
        writePowerRecord()

        if (batteryVoltage < 3.5):
                print "--->>>>Time to Shutdown<<<<---"
                shutdownPi("low voltage shutdown")

# every 15 minutes, build new graphs

if ((secondCount % (15*60)) == 0):
        # print every 900 seconds
        sampleAndDisplay()

# every 48 hours, reboot
if ((secondCount % (60*60*48)) == 0):
        # reboot every 48() hours
        rebootPi("48 hour reboot")

secondCount = secondCount + 1
# reset secondCount to prevent overflow forever

if (secondCount == 1000001):
        secondCount = 1

time.sleep(1.0)
```

Note that we reboot the Pi every two days. Why do we do that? We have noticed that after heavy usage of MatPlotLib and/or MySQL, that sometimes after a long time, you run out of resources, giving all sorts of odd behavior. Since the RaspberryPi A+ has a small amount of RAM, rebooting is the easiest way of fixing it.

Check out all the code up on github.com [https://github.com/switchdoclabs/WeatherPi].

The code for the RasPiConnect [www.milocreek.com/] control panel is discussed in the next section.

The RasPiConnect Control Panel

I use RasPiConnect to build our control panels for our projects. It allows us to put graphs, controls, buttons, sliders, etc., up on our iPad/iPhone screens without having to write apps. RasPiConnect works on Raspberry Pi's and on Arduinos. We have used this software on five different projects, with IOTWeatherPi being the latest.

How to build a control panel for IOTWeatherPi is beyond the scope of this chapter, but here is the tutorial [www.switchdoc.com/?p=523] that we wrote for doing what we are doing for IOTWeatherPi. We are using the same command-passing mechanism in IOTWeatherPi that we used in MouseAir. RasPiConnect comes with an excellent, comprehensive manual here [www.milocreek.com/wiki/index.php/Main_Page].

All the RasPiConnect code that we used in IOTWeatherPi is on github under github.com/switchdoclabs [https://github.com/switchdoclabs/WeatherPi-RasPiConnect]. Note that only the directory local is uploaded as that is the only place changes to the code are made as explained in the RasPiConnect manual.

The IOTWeatherPi has been outside for about 16 weeks now. Working perfectly. You can see the box being charged up and then going to battery power as the sun moves behind the house. We have had hot days and cold nights as we are just starting to move out of spring into summer. It is not quite generating enough electricity to run 24 hours at the moment (because it is in the shade until 9 a.m. and after about 3 p.m. - not quite 8 hours of sun). This will be fixed when I move it up to the top of the house where it will have sun about 12 hours a day on average (when the sun is not behind clouds!). Figure 3-21 shows the graph of the solar power performance after a week of sunshine.

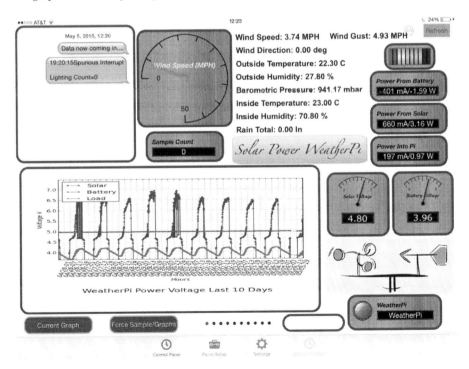

Figure 3-21. IOTWeatherPi Control Panel

Improvements

We aren't building graphs for the Wind Speed, Direction, and Rain yet. We are just reporting the current values on the RasPiConnect control panel. All the data is being saved into MySQL, however.

The temperature and lightning displays need to be fixed and improved.

The cool thing is that all of this can be done remotely!

Tweeting Your Weather Data

Tweeting is a great way of reading short messages from people with little to say. With the IOT IOTWeatherPi, you can join this epic project to be in on the fun. Of course, some people do have interesting things to say and now you can start tweeting IOT weather information. You may not have a lot of followers, but you can follow your IOT IOTWeatherPi from anywhere!

Getting Started

The first thing to do is install the Twython software [https://twython.readthedocs.org/en/latest/]. This is a Python library that will allow your application to post new Tweets and interact with Twitter outside of the Twitter web site.

Copy and paste these commands one at a time on your Raspberry Pi. Most of these require an answer to continue. The first two (update/upgrade) are general commands that update your Raspberry Pi to the latest and greatest software. A good thing to do in general.

```
sudo apt-get update
sudo apt-get upgrade
sudo apt-get install python-setuptools
sudo apt-get install python-dev
sudo easy_install pip
sudo pip install twython
sudo apt-get install libffi-dev libssl-dev
sudo pip install --upgrade pyopenssl ndg-httpsclient pyasn1 pip
sudo pip install requests
```

Now we have Twython installed on your IOTWeatherPi. Figure 3-22 shows an iPhone screenshot of the resulting Tweets.

Figure 3-22. IOTWeatherPi Tweeting

Registering a Twitter App

The Twitter API (Application Programming Interface) is a REST interface. A REST (Representational State Transfer) interface is a software architecture style for building scalable web services.

RESTful systems typically, but not always (and specifically does regarding the Twitter Interface), communicate over the Internet with the same HTTP verbs (GET, POST, PUT, DELETE, etc.), which web browsers use to retrieve web pages and to send data to remote servers.

The first thing you need to do is set up a new Twitter account for your project. In general, you don't want to tweet your temperature and things through your personal account and to all your followers. Doing that is a great way to get de-followed very quickly. Go to Twitter and do that now. When you have done that, move to the next paragraph.

In order to use the Twitter API, you will need to register a new application (your IOTWeatherPi in this case). Do that from this link [https://apps.twitter.com/app/new] – no need to specify a callback URL, and just make up a web site if you like. Figure 3-23 shows the initial application screen.

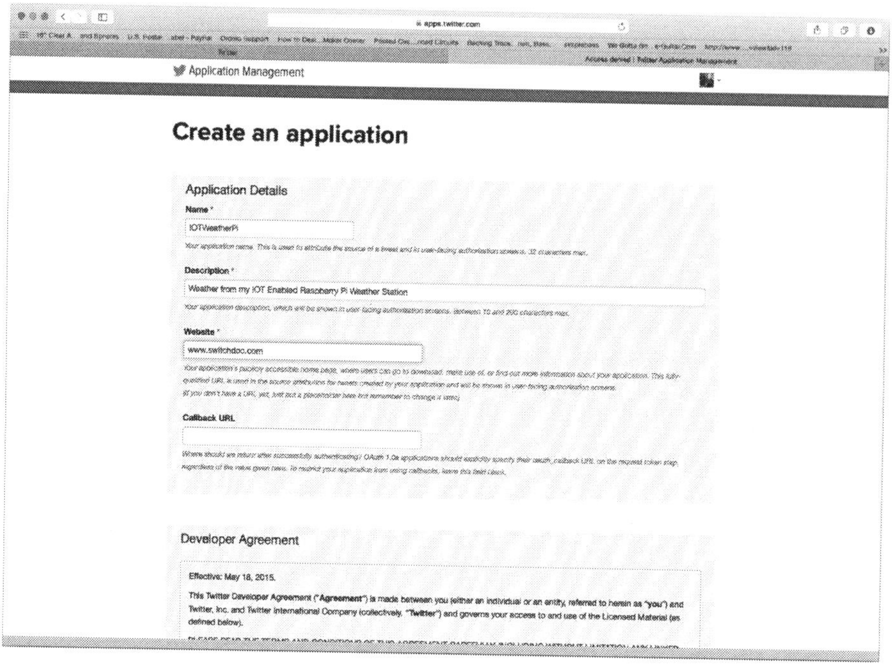

Figure 3-23. *Twitter Application Screen*

Next, go to the Keys and Access Tokens and create an Access Token. Keep this page open. You will need to put the tokens in your application.

Look in the Twitter subdirectory in the IOTWeatherPi software directory and edit the twitter.py file to add your ACCESS_KEY (which is the Access Token on the Twitter page).

```
#!/usr/bin/env python

# twitter.py
# SwitchDoc Labs
# 07/23/15

import sys

import datetime

from twython import Twython
```

```
def sendTweet(twitter, tweetString):
        # if conflocal.py is not found, import default conf.py

        # Check for user imports
        try:
                import conflocal as conf
        except ImportError:
                import conf

        today = datetime.datetime.utcnow()
        datestring = today.strftime("%H:%M:%S UTC:")

        try:
                sendString = datestring + tweetString
                twitter.update_status(status=sendString)
                return 0

        except:
                return 1
```

Following is the initialization code in WeatherPi.py:

```
# setup twitter
from twython import Twython

import twitter

twitterObject = Twython(conf.CONSUMER_KEY,conf.CONSUMER_SECRET,conf.ACCESS_
TOKEN,conf.ACCESS_TOKEN_SECRET)
```

You put the initialization codes (CONSUMER_KEY, etc.) into conf.py from the Twitter development page.

Here is the code in IOTWeatherPi that does the temperature and humidity tweet every 30 minutes:

```
        # every 30 minutes, check wifi connections and tweet

        if ((secondCount % (30*60)) == 0):
                # print every 900 seconds
                WLAN_check()

                # send tweet
                tweetString = "OutsideTemp: %0.1fC OutsideHum: %0.1f%%
                Wind: %0.1fKPH" % (outsideTemperature, outsideHumidity,
                currentWindSpeed * 1.6)

                twitter.sendTweet(twitterObject, tweetString)
```

And the lightning warning tweet:

```
twitter.sendTweet(twitterObject,  "IOTWeatherPi Lightning Detected"
+ str(distance) + "km away.")
```

Now your IOTWeatherPi is connected to Twitter. Next, we will set up the
IOTWeatherPi to text us the same information.

Texting Your Weather Data

Texting from your WeatherPi is much simpler than even tweeting. The key is to figure
out what carrier you are texting to and incorporate the gateway in your e-mail address
(Table 3-5).

Table 3-5. *Text Messaging E-Mail Addresses*

Carrier	E-Mail to SMS gateway
Alltel	[insert 10-digit number] @message.alltel.com
AT&T	[insert 10-digit number] @txt.att.net
Boost Mobile	[insert 10-digit number] @myboostmobile.com
Sprint	[insert 10-digit number] @messaging.sprintpcs.com
T-Mobile	[insert 10-digit number] @tmomail.net
US Cellular	[insert 10-digit number] @email.uscc.net
Verizon	[insert 10-digit number] @vtext.com
Virgin Mobile	[insert 10-digit number] @vmobl.com

More carriers and gateways are listed here [citation https://en.wikipedia.org/
wiki/SMS_gateway]

The code for texting is thus the same as the code for sending e-mails.

Here is the code for sending e-mails in IOTWeatherPi:

```
def sendEmail(source, message, subject, toaddress, fromaddress, filename):
    # if conflocal.py is not found, import default conf.py

    # Check for user imports
    try:
        import conflocal as conf
    except ImportError:
        import conf

    # Import smtplib for the actual sending function
    import smtplib
```

```python
# Here are the email package modules we'll need
from email.mime.image import MIMEImage
from email.mime.multipart import MIMEMultipart
from email.mime.text import MIMEText

COMMASPACE = ', '

# Create the container (outer) email message.
msg = MIMEMultipart()
msg['Subject'] = subject
# me == the sender's email address
# family = the list of all recipients' email addresses
msg['From'] = fromaddress
msg['To'] =  toaddress
#msg.attach(message)

mainbody = MIMEText(message, 'plain')
msg.attach(mainbody)

# Assume we know that the image files are all in PNG format
# Open the files in binary mode.  Let the MIMEImage class
automatically
# guess the specific image type.
if (filename != ""):
        fp = open(filename, 'rb')
        img = MIMEImage(fp.read())
        fp.close()
        msg.attach(img)

# Send the email via our own SMTP server.

try:
        # open up a line with the server
        s = smtplib.SMTP("smtp.gmail.com", 587)
        s.ehlo()
        s.starttls()
        s.ehlo()

        # login, send email, logout
        s.login(conf.mailUser, conf.mailPassword)
        s.sendmail(conf.mailUser, toaddress, msg.as_string())
        #s.close()

        s.quit()

except:

        print("sendmail exception raised")
    return 0
```

Note that the addresses for to and from are defined in conf.py along with the Twitter information.

And here is the single line of code to send a lightning warning text message:

```
sendemail.sendEmail("test", "IOTWeatherPi Lightning Detected\n",
as3935LastStatus, conf.textnotifyAddress,  conf.textfromAddress, "");
```

Figure 3-24 shows that a set of text messages was delivered to me in Curacao from 3,500 miles away from our IOTWeatherPi at SwitchDoc Labs.

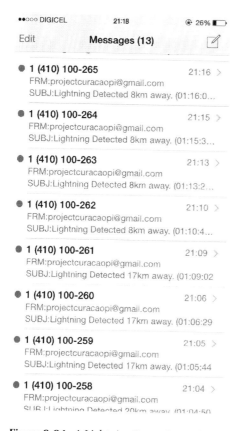

Figure 3-24. *A Lightning Storm Moves by SwitchDoc Labs*

Supplying Your Data to the World - CWOP

There are a number of web sites and companies that would love you to send them your weather data. Two of these are CWOP and WeatherUnderground. For the purposes of this project, we will send the data to CWOP (Citizens Weather Observation Program).

CWOP

The Citizen Weather Observer Program (CWOP) is a network of privately owned electronic weather stations concentrated in the United States but also located in over 150 countries. Network participation allows volunteers with computerized weather stations to send automated surface weather observations to the National Weather Service. This data is then used by the Rapid Refresh forecast model to produce short-term forecasts (3 to 12 hours into the future) of conditions across the United States' lower 48 states.

CWOP Observations are also redistributed to the public.

The CWOP was originally set up by amateur radio operators experimenting with packet radio, but now contains a majority of Internet-only connected stations. As of July 2015, more than 10,000 stations worldwide report regularly to the CWOP network.

CWOP Software Interface to IOTWeatherPi

When you talk to the CWOP server, you use a protocol called APRS (Automatic Packet Reporting System).

APRS was originally an amateur radio-based system for real-time communications of information of immediate value in the local area. Now it is used in a number of applications where data packets need to be disseminated to multiple locations.

The software that I am using in this project is based on the excellent work of Tom Hayward and his pywxtd project [https://github.com/kd7lxl/pywxtd]. We have removed the weather station parsing code and the daemon code and are just using the APRS libraries to send the data to CWOP.

CWOP Software

The CWOP software reads data from the IOTWeather station and sends an APRS packet to the CWOP servers with our current weather data.

First is the post_CWOP code used to send the packet to the CWOP servers. We install the CWOP code in the main IOTWeatherPi loop to fire every 15 minutes:

```
# every 15 minutes, build new graphs

if ((secondCount % (15*60)) == 0):
        # print every 900 seconds
        sampleWeather()
        sampleSunAirPlus()
        doAllGraphs.doAllGraphs()
        # send our CWOP data
```

```
# wind direction - degrees from true north
# wind speed - integer MPH
# wind gust - integer MPH
# temperature - degrees F
# rain since midnight - hundredths of inches
# humidity - % where 100% = 00
# pressure - 5 numbers in tenths of millibars

CWOP.post_CWOP(wind_dir=currentWindDirection, wind_
speed=currentWindSpeed, wind_gust=currentWindGust, temperat
ure=CtoFInteger(outsideTemperature), rain_since_midnight=0,
humidity=convertHumidity(outsideHumidity), pressure=int(bmp1
80SeaLevel*100+0.5))
```

Next, we have the code we use to construct the CWOP APRS packets:

```
#!/usr/bin/env python

# SwitchDoc Labs
# July 24, 2015
# Version 1.0

"""
initially from Tom Hayward
builds and submits an
APRS weather packet to the APRS-IS/CWOP.
BSD License and stuff
Copyright 2010 Tom Hayward <tom@tomh.us>
"""
import sys, os, time
from datetime import datetime, timedelta

from socket import *

sys.path.append('..')

# Check for user imports
try:
        import conflocal as conf
except ImportError:
        import conf
```

```python
def make_aprs_wx(wind_dir=None, wind_speed=None, wind_gust=None,
temperature=None, rain_since_midnight=None, humidity=None, pressure=None):
    """
    Assembles the payload of the APRS weather packet.
    """
    def str_or_dots(number, length):
        """
        If parameter is None, fill space with dots. Else, zero-pad.
        """
        if number is None:
            return '.'*length
        else:
            format_type = {
                'int': 'd',
                'float': '.0f',
            }[type(number).__name__]
            return ''.join(('%0',str(length),format_type)) % number

    timeStringZulu = time.strftime("%d%H%M")
    return '@%sz%s/%s_%s/%sg%st%sP%sh%sb%s%s' % (
        timeStringZulu,
        conf.STATIONLATITUDE,
        conf.STATIONLONGITUDE,
        str_or_dots(wind_dir, 3),
        str_or_dots(wind_speed, 3),
        str_or_dots(wind_gust, 3),
        str_or_dots(temperature, 3),
        str_or_dots(rain_since_midnight, 3),
        str_or_dots(humidity, 2),
        str_or_dots(pressure, 5),
        conf.STATION_TYPE
    )

def post_CWOP(wind_dir=None, wind_speed=None, wind_gust=None,
temperature=None, rain_since_midnight=None, humidity=None, pressure=None):

    # post to aprs
    wx = make_aprs_wx(wind_dir=wind_dir, wind_speed=wind_speed, wind_
gust=wind_gust, temperature=temperature, rain_since_midnight=rain_since_
midnight, humidity=humidity, pressure=pressure)

    print time.strftime("%Y-%m-%d %H:%M:%S"), wx

    send_aprs(conf.APRS_HOST, conf.APRS_PORT, conf.APRS_USER, conf.
APRS_PASS, conf.CALLSIGN, wx)

    return
```

107

Example CWOP Packet

I had a difficult time figuring out exactly what format of APRS to send. Here is an example of the actual packets we send:

```
EW7667>APRS,TCPIP:@251954z4739.22N/11705.11W_158/004g006t076P000h49b01015IO
TWeatherPi
```

Results

Here is the packet and data as received by the CWOP server rom IOTWeatherPi (our CWOP registration number is EW7667). Now we are connected to the IOT for weather stations!

Here are some of the recorded packets from finds.com:

```
EW7667>APRS,TCPXX*,qAX,CWOP-3:@252056z4739.22N/11705.11W_045/009g013t075P000
h46b10147IOTWeatherPi
EW7667>APRS,TCPXX*,qAX,CWOP-3:@252116z4739.22N/11705.11W_045/010g036t077P000
h44b10146IOTWeatherPi
EW7667>APRS,TCPXX*,qAX,CWOP-3:@252135z4739.22N/11705.11W_045/008g006t077P000
h42b10143IOTWeatherPi
```

When you have collected a lot of data, findu.com will display some cool graphs as shown in `findu.com`. See Figure 3-25 [`www.findu.com/cgi-bin/wxpage.cgi?call=EW766`
`7&last=48&radar=***`].

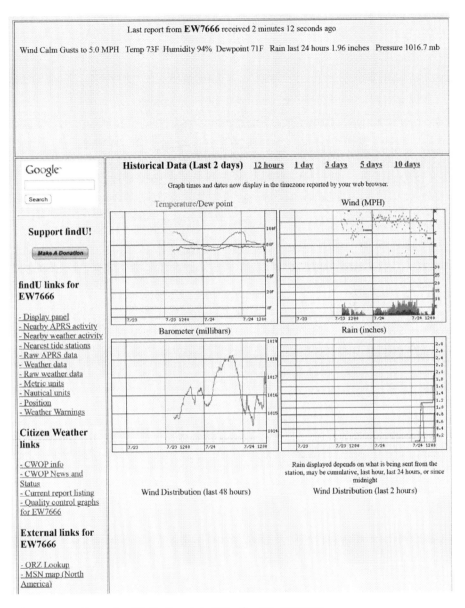

Figure 3-25. Example of Fully Populated Weather Site EW7666

Conclusion

In Figure 3-26, we show the IOTWeatherPi with the optional Lightning Pylon out in the wild [www.instructables.com/id/Lightning-Detector-for-Raspberry-Pi-WeatherPi-Weat/].

Figure 3-26. *IOTWeatherPi Deployed*

It is amazing what you can do with hardware such as the Raspberry Pi and off-the-shelf sensors to sense the environment. With a CPLPFC rating of 6, IOTWeatherPi is probably not a commercially deployable system in the IOT, but it is a great base unit to experiment with and get familiar with hardware and software for the IOT.

Here are some additional ideas for projects based on IOTWeatherPi:

- Replacing the WiFi with a GSM data connection - This would use the Cellular Data Network for communications.

- Make a custom Facebook posting with your weather - This would use the Facebook API to make automated postings, much like Twitter.

- Adding a GPS receiver and storing that data. You now have a mobile weather station! When it gets back to WiFi, all the stored data will be available. You could tweet your location and the local conditions on the fly with a GSM connection.

- Adding additional air quality sensors, UV sensors, dust sensors. You have a lot of input / output pins and I2C addressing space that you can fill with more interesting sensors.

The main power expense in IOTWeatherPi is the Raspberry Pi. By replacing the Raspberry Pi with a small Arduino (and dramatically reducing the functionality - Arduinos aren't anywhere near as powerful as the combination of the Raspberry Pi and Linux), you could improve your CPLPFC rating substantially.

Next? We move on to using the Raspberry Pi to detect iBeacons and figure out where you are when you carry the RaspberryPi around with you. With IOTBeaconAir, we will modify the lights using Philips Hue lights to light your way.

CHAPTER 4

■ ■ ■

Changing Your Environment with IOT and iBeacons

Chapter Goal: Gather Location Data on Your IOT device: Locate Where You Are and Deliver Location Dependent Data and Conduct Actions on Where You Are

Topics Covered in This Chapter:

- iBeacons and how can you use them
- Detecting and reading iBeacons from the Raspberry Pi
- Finding your location – Trilateralization in a fuzzy world
- Displaying your Location on a Control Panel
- Turning lights off and on by your location

In Chapter 3, you saw a flexible, solar powered system to deliver data to the IOT (in this case including the National Oceanic and Atmospheric Administration (NOAA) through the weather interface, CWOP. IOTWeatherPi delivered a lot of information on a regular basis.

In this chapter, we take our new IOT device, IOTBeaconAir, to another level. Now we are collecting less information (and even sending less to the IOT), but we are taking data on the environment (where you are) and using it to change the environment (the amount of lighting where you are). This takes us to quite another level of interaction with the IOT.

The IOTBeaconAir

IOTBeaconAir is a portable Raspberry Pi based project that reads the "advertising" packets emitted by iBeacons, roughly calculates your position, and then turns on lights that are close to you. The Pi then calculates the brightness based on just how close you are. The idea is that you can walk around your house with your Pi and the lights will follow you.

In other words, I am using iBeacons to figure out where my portable Pi is physically located (in a pouch on my hip as I walk around the house) and then I control various devices with the Pi.

© John C. Shovic 2016

J. C. Shovic, *Raspberry Pi IoT Projects*, DOI 10.1007/978-1-4842-1377-3_4

The unique aspect of IOTBeaconAir versus the many other extant Pi based iBeacon projects is that I am not programming the Raspberry Pi to be an iBeacon; I am doing the opposite. I am using the Pi to read other iBeacons. I am using specialized iBeacons in this project, but you could also build your own iBeacons out of Raspberry Pi's and then read them via Bluetooth with this project.

This project is based around a portable Raspberry Pi ModelB connected with a Bluetooth 4.0 USB dongle and a Wi-Pi Wireless USB dongle. The completed IOTBeaconAir Portable Pi project is shown in Figure 4-1.

Figure 4-1. *IOTBeaconAir Portable Pi*

IOT Characterization of This Project

As I discussed in Chapter 1, the first thing to do to understand an IOT project is to look at our six different aspects of IOT. IOTBeaconAir is a much simpler project than IOTWeatherPi. Table 4-1 shows our six components.

Table 4-1. *Components of the IOTBeaconAir Project*

IOTBeaconAir Characterization (CPLPFC)		
Aspect	Rating	Comments
Communications	9	WiFi connection to Internet - can do AdHoc mesh-type communication and Bluetooth
Processor Power	8	Raspberry Pi B+ / 256Mb RAM
Local Storage	8	8GB of SD Card
Power Consumption	1	~300mA consumption - Not reasonable for small batteries
Functionality	8	Full Linux-based system. MySQL, etc.
Cost	1	Expensive for many applications. Board is ~$25+

Ratings are from 1–10, 1 being the least suitable for IOT and 10 being the most suitable for IOT applications.

This gives us a CPLPFC rating of 5.8, a little less than IOTWeatherPi (6). Great for learning, not so good for deployment for most applications.

No doubt about it, the Raspberry Pi is a very flexible and powerful IOT platform. However, the power consumption, cost, and physical size of the device make it more suitable for prototyping or for stand-alone highly functional IOT units.

How Does This Device Hook Up to the IOT?

With IOTBeaconAir, like the previous chapter, we have a lot of options. We can hook up to the Internet using the WiFi connector. We can use the Bluetooth to hook up to local devices, and we can also use the WiFi in AdHoc mode to make local connections. In this chapter, we will be using the WiFi interface to talk to the wider world of IOT devices.

Hardware List

Following is a list of the hardware you'll need in order to build this project:

- Raspberry Pi Model B+
- Adafruit USB Battery Pack for Raspberry Pi - 10000mAh - 2 x 5V @ 2A
- Estimote Beacons Developer Kit
- KST Technologies Particle iBeacons
- IOGear Bluetooth 4.0 USB Micro Adapter - Model GBU521
- Wi-Pi Raspberry Pi 802.11n Wireless Adapter

iBeacons

iBeacon is the Apple trademark for a low-powered Bluetooth device. An iBeacon is a low-powered, low-cost transmitter that can notify nearby devices of their presence and a rough approximation of range. There are a number of manufacturers that are producing these devices and most smartphones (and Raspberry Pi's!) can be made to act as an iBeacon. It uses Bluetooth Low Energy (BLE), also known as Bluetooth Smart iBeacons can also be received on Bluetooth 4.0 devices that support dual mode (such as the IOGear dongle specified above). Note that receiving iBeacons on a generic Bluetooth dongle can be quite problematic. Stick with the IOGear Model GBU521 if you can.

Applications of iBeacons include location-aware advertising, social media check-ins, or notifications sent to your smartphone or Pi. An iBeacon transmits an advertising packet containing an UDID (Unique Device Identifier) that identifies the manufacturer and then a major and minor number that can be used to identify the specific device. It also sends out an RSSI (Relative Signal Strength Indicator) that can be used to approximate the distance to the iBeacon device.

It is important to note that almost all the logic behind an iBeacon deployment is through the supporting application on the device (a Raspberry Pi in our case). The only role of the iBeacon is to advertise to the device of its own existence at a physical location. In some cases, you can connect to an individual device through the iBeacon's GATT (General ATTribute profile) although some iBeacons have a proprietary interface (like the Estimote iBeacons) that prohibit this.

This requirement of having the application device (like a smartphone or Raspberry Pi) read and take actions on the position of the iBeacons remains a roadblock to widespread adoption of iBeacons in the marketplace. Doing it any other way (say for the iBeacons to detect your phone) is a big privacy concern and so things are likely to stay this way for the foreseeable future. See Chapter 7, "Computer Security and the IOT," for a number of reasons that this is a good thing.

The iBeacons we used are shown in Figure 4-2.

Figure 4-2. iBeacons

I used two types of iBeacons: Estimote and KS Technologies Particles. Both worked adequately with regard to receiving advertising packets, but the Estimote beacons have a proprietary interface that makes it not Linux and Raspberry Pi friendly, so I recommend the Particle iBeacons because you can read and write to the devices from the Raspberry Pi. The Estimote only supports a proprietary SDK on Android and iPhone. Of course, you can always roll your own iBeacon using a Raspberry Pi [www.wadewegner.com/2014/05/create-an-ibeacon-transmitter-with-the-raspberry-pi/]. The Particle iBeacon is shown in Figure 4-3.

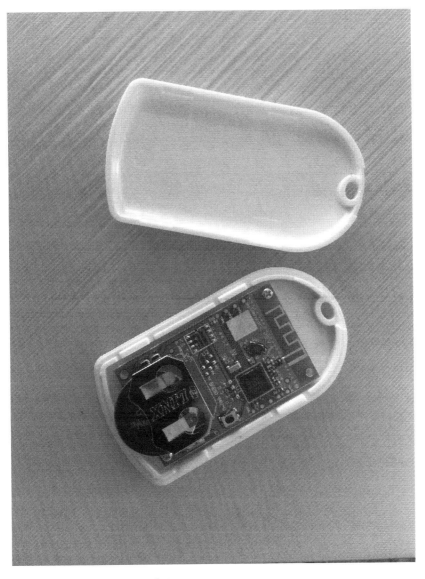

Figure 4-3. *Inside of a Particle iBeacon*

There are four major pieces of software in IOTBeaconAir: the Bluetooth iBeacon Scanner, the Philips Hue interface, the main IOTBeaconAir software, and the RasPiConnect Server software.

Bluetooth iBeacon Scanner

Technically, this was the most difficult part of the IOTBeaconAir system. The software available to do this was not very reliable and did not produce the kind of information I was interested in. Figure 4-4 shows the iBeacons near to my lab bench using the BTLExplorer App on my iPhone from KS Technologies.

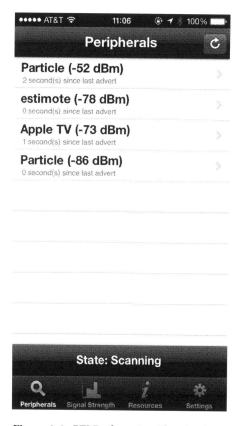

Figure 4-4. *BTLExplorer App Showing iBeacons*

Note that we are picking up on an Estimote beacon and two Particle beacons. Interestingly enough, we are also picking up an Apple TV located about 40 feet away. I was not aware that the Apple TV was broadcasting an iBeacon packet, but on checking it is used for an undocumented way of setting up the Apple TV from your iPhone. The numbers don't make a lot of sense in the iBeacon advertising packet, but that is a problem for another day.

The biggest issue with this project was to be able to reliably read iBeacon data from a Bluetooth Dongle (I'm using an IOGear Bluetooth 4.0 USB Micro Adapter - Model GBU521). A number of the methods out there on the Web were less than satisfactory (doing hcidump scans) and often ended up hanging the Bluetooth on the Pi, requiring a reboot. Once I went to using my software library, I have zero hang-ups and the software runs for days.

iBeacons use Bluetooth Low Energy (BLE) protocols to communicate, which is a relatively new type of Bluetooth and has spotty support. Finally I stumbled upon a program using blueZ (Linux Bluetooth Library) native calls, which with a lot of modifications, bug fixes, and cutting of code I didn't need, I had a iBeacon scanner that worked every time. I have posted my working version on the SwitchDoc Labs github (github.com/switchdoclabs/iBeacon-Scanner-) so you can download it and test your setup.

The blescan.py program is easy to test and use but requires some setup on the Raspberry Pi. See the section below on installing all the required software on the Raspberry Pi.

Here is the output from the programming running in SwitchDoc Labs. We have a lot of iBeacons sitting around.

```
pi@BeaconAir ~/blescanner $ sudo python testblescan.py
ble thread started
----------
cf:68:cc:c7:33:10,b9407f30f5f8466eaff925556b57fe6d,13072,52423,-74,-78
cf:68:cc:c7:33:10,74696d6f74650e160a181033c7cc68cf,46608,13255,-52,-77
da:f4:2e:a0:70:b1,b9407f30f5f8466eaff925556b57fe6d,28849,11936,-74,-79
da:f4:2e:a0:70:b1,74696d6f74650e160a18b170a02ef4da,46769,28832,46,-78
dd:5d:d3:35:09:dd,8aefb0316c32486f825be26fa193487d,1,1,-64,-78
c3:11:48:9b:cf:fa,8aefb0316c32486f825be26fa193487d,0,0,-64,-73
fd:5b:12:7f:02:e4,b9407f30f5f8466eaff925556b57fe6d,740,4735,-74,-79
fd:5b:12:7f:02:e4,74696d6f74650e160a18e4027f125bfd,46820,639,18,-80
dd:5d:d3:35:09:dd,8aefb0316c32486f825be26fa193487d,1,1,-64,-77
```

We are finding eight different iBeacons, which matches the actual count. Before you can do this, you need to install the latest version of bluez, the Bluetooth stack for the Raspberry Pi (instructions below). Note: You could use apt-get, but the apt-get version is old and has patchy support for iBeacons.

Phillips Hue Lighting System

The Phillips Hue lighting system is a Zigbee-based wireless way of controlling intensity, color combinations, and on/off from a Phillips Hub based on your local network. The standard apps for Android and iOS are very powerful, but for us Raspberry Pi people, the best part is that Phillips has released the API for the hub for the DIY crowd. It's somewhat expensive ($60/bulb) but robust and very easy to use and to hack. All commands are sent via wireless or Ethernet to the Phillips Hue Hub and the Hub communicates to the individual devices.

What Is Zigbee?

ZigBee is a joint specification for a suite of high-level communication protocols used to create personal area networks built from small, low-power digital radios. In this regard, it is very similar to Low Power Bluetooth. The transmission distance is limited to about 10–100 meters, depending on the power output and the transmission environment. The Phillips Hue ZigBee devices work well within a house, but sometimes you will see lights jump on and off the network in what seems to be humidity-related events. Given the frequencies and low-power characteristics of ZigBee, this could certainly be the case.

The ZigBee technology is meant to be simpler and less expensive than Bluetooth and WiFi, not only in dollar cost, but also processor overhead to deal with the communications channel. Just imagine what the processor has to do to interpret an incoming TCP/IP packet and get to the user data. ZigBee can be used without the really "heavy" protocol stack to communicate with local devices through a mesh network to reach more distant Zigbees (see Chapter 6) and then pass to a "beefier" processor, such as a Raspberry Pi to send information into the IOT on the Internet.

ZigBee is typically used in low-data rate IOT applications that require long battery life (a very important feature!) and secure networking. ZigBee networks are secured by 128-bit symmetric encryption keys. See Chapter 7 for a discussion of encryption keys. ZigBee has a defined rate of 250 kbit/s, which is not very fast for web access but you can send a lot of data with that speed.

The ZigBee name refers to the waggle dance of honey bees after their return to the beehive.

Phillips Hue Hub

The Phillips Hue hub communicates via authenticated JSON packets. There are a number of Python packages designed for communication with the Phillips Hue Hub. We chose to use one written by Studio Imaginaire (studioimaginaire.com/en) called phue. It is a group of smart French people that did a great job producing the phue library. Considering the IOTBeaconAir logo was designed in France, it seemed appropriate to use this library. You can download it at github.com/studioimaginaire/phue. See installation instructions below.

Our test rooms for IOTBeaconAir has 10 Phillips Hue A19 Standard bulbs, 3 Phillips Hue BR-30 down wash lights, and 2 Phillips Friends of Hue Bloom lights. It was expensive but worth it (the A19 bulbs are $60 apiece, BR30 bulbs $60 apiece, and the Blooms are $80 apiece). These prices should decrease in the future.

BeaconAir Hardware, Software, and Configuration

To work with the BeaconAir, you need to know about the hardware and software. You also need to know about how the software is configured. The following subsections cover each of these topics.

BeaconAir Hardware Description

The IOTBeaconAir hardware is pretty straightforward. We use a stock Raspberry Model B+ with a Wi-Pi WiFi USB dongle and an IOGear Bluetooth 4.0 USB dongle. Everything else is done in software. Figure 4-5 shows the system, as well as showing how iBeacons that allow us to find the approximate physical position of our IOTBeaconAir Portable Pi.

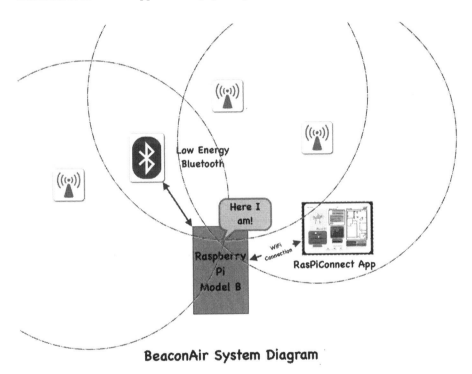

Figure 4-5. IOTBeaconAir System Diagram

BeaconAir Software Description

The IOTBeaconAir software consists of four major pieces. I have described the iBeacon Scanner and the Phillips Hue Python library phue above. The two major pieces remaining are the main program loop and the RasPiConnect Local.py / control panel.

The IOTBeaconAir software block diagram is shown in Figure 4-6.

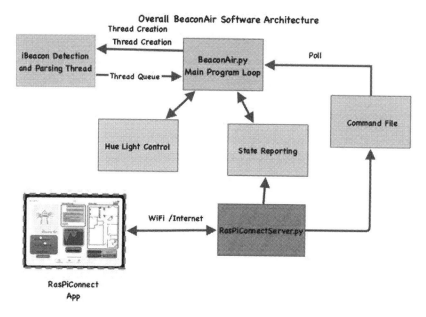

Figure 4-6. *IOTBeaconAir Software Block Diagram*

The main software runs in a loop, with a sleep of 0.25 seconds at the end. It checks for two sources of work. First it checks a queue that is connected to the iBeacon Scanning software running in a background thread. If the queue is empty, we have no new iBeacon reports so we go down and check to see if there are commands waiting from the RasPiConnect control panel.

```
if (queueBLE.empty() == False):
        result = queueBLE.get(False)

    # process commands from RasPiConnect
        processCommand()
```

If the queue has iBeacon results to deliver, we then go through the main loop and process the iBeacon information, set various informational parameters, build the new web page to deliver to RasPiConnect, and control the lights.

I have removed the debugging information to make things clearer. All calculations are done in meters and converted to pixels for display.

The first thing we do is process the incoming iBeacon list to fill our beacon arrays. We then clear out old values.

```
result = queueBLE.get(False)
```

```
utils.processiBeaconList(result,currentiBeaconRSSI, currentiBeaconTimeStamp,
rollingiBeaconRSSI)
utils.clearOldValues(10,currentiBeaconRSSI, currentiBeaconTimeStamp,rolling
iBeaconRSSI)
```

Next we calculate the current IOTBeaconAir physical position but only if we have greater than three beacons.

```
# update position
if (utils.haveThreeGoodBeacons(rollingiBeaconRSSI) >= 3):
        oldbeacons = beacons
        beacons = utils.get3ClosestBeacons(rollingiBeaconRSSI)
        if (cmp(oldbeacons, beacons) != 0):
bubblelog.writeToBubbleLog("closebeacons:%i,%i,%i" % (beacons[0],
beacons[1], beacons[2]))
        myPosition = utils.XgetXYFrom3Beacons
        (beacons[0],beacons[1],beacons[2], rollingiBeaconRSSI)
```

I now have the latest calculated position. Next I calculate the jitter in the position. A big value of jitter says either you are moving or there are significant amounts of noise in the iBeacon reports or both.

```
# calculate jitter in position
jitter = (((lastPosition[0] - myPosition[0])/lastPosition[0]) +
((lastPosition[1] - myPosition[1])/lastPosition[1]))/2.0
jitter = jitter * 100.0    # to get to percent
lastPosition = myPosition
```

Now I write out the jitter for RasPiconnect to read and send to the jitter graph on the control panel.

```
f = open("/home/pi/BeaconAir/state/distancejitter.txt", "w")
```

```
f.write(str(jitter))
f.close()
```

Next I calculate the distance from my position to all the lights and then turn the light on, change brightness, or turn it off depending on the distance.

```
lights.checkForLightTrigger(myPosition, LIGHT_DISTANCE_SENSITIVITY,
LIGHT_BRIGHTNESS_SENSITIVITY, currentLightState)
```

Next the web page is built for display on RasPiConnect.

```
# build webpage
webmap.buildWebMapToFile(myPosition, rollingiBeaconRSSI, currentLightState,
DISPLAY_BEACON_ON, DISPLAY_LIGHTS_ON)
```

Finally, I update the current beacon count and build the graph for display on RasPiConnect.

```
# build beacon count graph

iBeaconChart.iBeacondetect(rollingiBeaconRSSI)
else:
# lost position
myPosition = [-myPosition[0], -myPosition[1]]
```

That is the entire main program for IOTBeaconAir.
Following is the full listing of the main program of IOTBeaconAir:

```
#!/usr/bin/python

# BeaconAir - Reads iBeacons and controls HUE lights
# SwitchDoc Labs February 2016
#
#
import sys
import time
import utils

sys.path.append('./ble')
sys.path.append('./config')

# if conflocal.py is not found, import default conf.py

# Check for user imports
try:
        import conflocal as conf
except ImportError:
        import conf

import bleThread

import lights
import webmap
import bubblelog
import iBeaconChart
```

```python
from threading import Thread
from Queue import Queue

# State Variables

currentiBeaconRSSI=[]
rollingiBeaconRSSI=[]
currentiBeaconTimeStamp=[]

# Light State Variables

currentLightState= []

LIGHT_BRIGHTNESS_SENSITIVITY = 2.0
LIGHT_DISTANCE_SENSITIVITY = 2.0
BEACON_ON = True
DISPLAY_BEACON_ON = True
DISPLAY_LIGHTS_ON = True

# init state variables
for beacon in conf.BeaconList:
        currentiBeaconRSSI.append(0)
        rollingiBeaconRSSI.append(0)
        currentiBeaconTimeStamp.append(time.time())

# init light state variables
for light in conf.LightList:
        currentLightState.append(0)

lights.initializeHue('192.168.1.6')

lights.setInitialLightState(currentLightState)

# recieve commands from RasPiConnect Execution Code

def completeCommand():

        f = open("/home/pi/BeaconAir/state/BeaconAirCommand.txt", "w")
        f.write("DONE")
        f.close()

def processCommand():
        global LIGHT_BRIGHTNESS_SENSITIVITY
        global LIGHT_DISTANCE_SENSITIVITY
        global BEACON_ON
        global DISPLAY_BEACON_ON
        global DISPLAY_LIGHTS_ON
        global currentLightState
```

```
f = open("/home/pi/BeaconAir/state/BeaconAirCommand.txt", "r")
command = f.read()
f.close()

if (command == "") or (command == "DONE"):
        # Nothing to do
        return False

# Check for our commands

print "Processing Command: ", command

if (command == "BEACONON"):
        BEACON_ON = True
        completeCommand()
        return True

if (command == "BEACONOFF"):
        BEACON_ON = False
        completeCommand()
        return True

if (command == "ALLLIGHTSON"):
        lights.allLights(True, currentLightState )
        completeCommand()
        return True

if (command == "ALLLIGHTSOFF"):
        lights.allLights(False, currentLightState)
        completeCommand()
        return True

if (command == "BEACONON"):
        BEACON_ON = True
        completeCommand()
        return True

if (command == "BEACONOFF"):
        BEACON_ON = False
        completeCommand()
        return True

if (command == "DISPLAYBEACONON"):
        DISPLAY_BEACON_ON = True
        completeCommand()
        return True
```

```
if (command == "DISPLAYBEACONOFF"):
        DISPLAY_BEACON_ON = False
        completeCommand()
        return True

if (command == "DISPLAYLIGHTSON"):
        DISPLAY_LIGHTS_ON = True
        completeCommand()
        return True

if (command == "DISPLAYLIGHTSOFF"):
        DISPLAY_LIGHTS_ON = False
        completeCommand()
        return True

if (command == "UPDATESENSITIVITIES"):

        try:
                f = open("/home/pi/BeaconAir/state/
                distanceSensitivity.txt", "r")
                commandresponse = f.read()
                LIGHT_DISTANCE_SENSITIVITY = float(commandresponse)
                f.close()
        except:
                LIGHT_DISTANCE_SENSITIVITY = 2.0

        try:
                f = open("/home/pi/BeaconAir/state/
                brightnessSensitivity.txt", "r")
                commandresponse - f.read()
                f.close()
                LIGHT_BRIGHTNESS_SENSITIVITY = float(commandresponse)
        except:
                LIGHT_BRIGHTNESS_SENSITIVITY = 2.0
        print "LIGHT_DISTANCE_SENSITIVITY, LIGHT_BRIGHTNESS_
SENSITIVITY= ", LIGHT_DISTANCE_SENSITIVITY, LIGHT_BRIGHTNESS_SENSITIVITY
        completeCommand()
        return True

completeCommand()
return True
```

```
# build configuration Table

# set up BLE thread
# set up a communication queue

queueBLE = Queue()
BLEThread = Thread(target=bleThread.bleDetect, args=(__name__,10,queueBLE,))
BLEThread.daemon = True
BLEThread.start()


bubblelog.writeToBubbleLog("BeaconAir Started")

# the main loop of BeaconAir
myPosition = [0,0]
lastPosition = [1,1]
beacons = []
while True:
        if (BEACON_ON == True):
                # check for iBeacon Updates
                print "Queue Length =", queueBLE.qsize()
                if (queueBLE.empty() == False):
                        result = queueBLE.get(False)
                        print "------"

                        utils.processiBeaconList(result,currentiBeaconRSSI,
                        currentiBeaconTimeStamp,rollingiBeaconRSSI)
                        utils.clearOldValues(10,currentiBeaconRSSI, currenti
                        BeaconTimeStamp,rollingiBeaconRSSI)
                        for beacon in conf.BeaconList:
                                utils.printBeaconDistance(beacon,
                                currentiBeaconRSSI, currentiBeaconTimeStamp,
                                rollingiBeaconRSSI)
                        # update position
                        if (utils.haveThreeGoodBeacons(rollingiBeaconRSSI)
                        >= 3):
                                oldbeacons = beacons
                                beacons = utils.get3ClosestBeacons(rollingi
                                BeaconRSSI)
                                print "beacons=", beacons
                                if (cmp(oldbeacons, beacons) != 0):

                                        bubblelog.writeToBubbleLog("close
                                        beacons:%i,%i,%i" % (beacons[0],
                                        beacons[1], beacons[2]))

                                        # setup for Kludge
                                        #rollingiBeaconRSSI[7] =
                                        rollingiBeaconRSSI[6]
```

```
myPosition = utils.getXYFrom3Beacon
s(beacons[0],beacons[1],beacons[2],
rollingiBeaconRSSI)
print "myPosition1 = %3.2f,%3.2f" %
(myPosition[0], myPosition[1])
#bubblelog.writeToBubbleLog("position
updated:%3.2f,%3.2f" % (myPosition[0],
myPosition[1]))

# calculate jitter in position
jitter = (((lastPosition[0] -
myPosition[0])/lastPosition[0]) +
((lastPosition[1] - myPosition[1])/
lastPosition[1]))/2.0
jitter = jitter * 100.0   # to get to
percent
lastPosition = myPosition
print "jitter=", jitter

f = open("/home/pi/BeaconAir/state/
distancejitter.txt", "w")

f.write(str(jitter))
f.close()

for light in conf.LightList:
        lightdistance = utils.
        distanceBetween
        TwoPoints([light[2],light[3]],
        myPosition)
        print "distance to light %i : %3.2f"
        % (light[0], lightdistance)
print "LIGHT_DISTANCE_SENSITIVITY, LIGHT_
BRIGHTNESS_SENSITIVITY= ", LIGHT_DISTANCE_
SENSITIVITY, LIGHT_BRIGHTNESS_SENSITIVITY
lights.checkForLightTrigger(myPositi
on, LIGHT_DISTANCE_SENSITIVITY, LIGHT_
BRIGHTNESS_SENSITIVITY, currentLightState)
print "DISPLAY_BEACON_ON, DISPLAY_LIGHTS_
ON", DISPLAY_BEACON_ON, DISPLAY_LIGHTS_ON
# build webpage
webmap.buildWebMapToFile(myPosition,
rollingiBeaconRSSI, currentLightState,
DISPLAY_BEACON_ON, DISPLAY_LIGHTS_ON)
```

```
                              # build beacon count graph

                              iBeaconChart.iBeacondetect(rollingiBeaconRSSI)
                    else:
                              # lost position
                              myPosition = [-myPosition[0],
                              -myPosition[1]]

          #print currentiBeaconRSSI
          #print currentiBeaconTimeStamp

# end of BEACON_ON - always process commands
else:
          if (queueBLE.empty() == False):
                    result = queueBLE.get(False)
          print "------"
          print "Beacon Disabled"
# process commands from RasPiConnect

processCommand()

time.sleep(0.25)
```

One very interesting part of IOTBeaconAir is building the HTML-based map showing position, beacons, and lights.

As I started this project, I felt that building this live map was going to be the biggest problem. I looked at building a live map with Matplotlib on the Pi, but it was computationally expensive and complicated. Then I looked at HTML drawing solutions and I found that it was almost trivial to do so. I used a Remote Webview in RasPiConnect for the control panel. Figure 4-7 shows the completed HTML map.

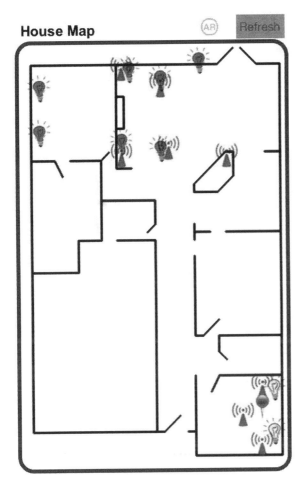

Figure 4-7. HTML House Map

To make this HTML map work, follow these steps:

1. Build a JPEG with the plan of your office or house. I took a picture of the house plans and then used GIMP [www.gimp.org] to draw the walls on the JPEG and then remove the JPEG layer. Worked like a champ. Then I had to measure a wall in meters and use GIMP to measure the same wall in pixels, and I had my meters to pixels constant (0.0375 m/px in my case). I put the 0,0 point at the top of the JPEG and then x is positive going to the right and y is positive down the left side.

2. In the configuration file, figure out the positions x,y for each of the lights and the beacon and put in the configuration file.

• Run the software. The resulting HTML code looks like the following:

```
<html><head><title></title><style>body,html,iframe{margin:0;padding:0;}
</style></head><body><div style='position: relative; left: 0; top: 0;'>
<img src='http://example.example.com:9600/static/mainplanfull.png'
style='position: relative; top: 0; left: 0;'/>
<img src='http://example.example.com:9600/static/iBeacon.png'
style='position: absolute; top: 490px; left: 299px;'/>
<img src='http://example.example.com:9600/static/iBeacon.png'
style='position: absolute; top: 19px; left: 122px;'/>
<img src='http://example.example.com:9600/static/iBeacon.png'
style='position: absolute; top: 127px; left: 122px;'/>
<img src='http://example.example.com:9600/static/iBeacon.png'
style='position: absolute; top: 40px; left: 173px;'/>
<img src='http://example.example.com:9600/static/iBeacon.png'
style='position: absolute; top: 118px; left: 183px;'/>
<img src='http://example.example.com:9600/static/iBeacon.png'
style='position: absolute; top: 128px; left: 257px;'/>
<img src='http://example.example.com:9600/static/iBeacon.png'
style='position: absolute; top: 418px; left: 300px;'/>
<img src='http://example.example.com:9600/static/iBeacon.png'
style='position: absolute; top: 453px; left: 275px;'/>
<img src='http://example.example.com:9600/static/OffLightBulb.png'
style='position: absolute; top: 418px; left: 315px;'/>
<img src='http://example.example.com:9600/static/OffLightBulb.png'
style='position: absolute; top: 473px; left: 315px;'/>
<img src='http://example.example.com:9600/static/OffLightBulb.png'
style='position: absolute; top: 19px; left: 132px;'/>
<img src='http://example.example.com:9600/static/OffLightBulb.png'
style='position: absolute; top: 30px; left: 173px;'/>
<img src='http://example.example.com:9600/static/OffLightBulb.png'
style='position: absolute; top: 118px; left: 173px;'/>
<img src='http://example.example.com:9600/static/OffLightBulb.png'
style='position: absolute; top: 109px; left: 122px;'/>
<img src='http://example.example.com:9600/static/OffLightBulb.png'
style='position: absolute; top: 8px; left: 222px;'/>
<img src='http://example.example.com:9600/static/OffLightBulb.png'
style='position: absolute; top: 42px; left: 16px;'/>
<img src='http://example.example.com:9600/static/OffLightBulb.png'
style='position: absolute; top: 98px; left: 16px;'/>
<img src='http://example.example.com:9600/static/red-pin.png'
style='position: absolute; top: 378px; left: 217px;'/>
</div></body></html>
```

This works like a champ. I made my icons with transparent backgrounds (again using GIMP).

BeaconAir Configuration File

The IOTBeaconAir Configuration file needs to be set up before the system can be used. It is located under config in the main directory. The three major parts of the configuration file are the following:

```
Scaling Factors
Beacon Configuration
Light Configuration
```

The following declarations show two of the scaling factors used in the project:

```
def pixelConv(pixels):
        return pixels * 0.0375      # in meters

def meterToPixel(meters):
        return int(meters / 0.0375)      # in pixels
```

Our beacon configuration is accomplished as follows:

```
# Beacon format:
#      BeaconNumber, LocalName, x, y, UDID, Major, Minor, Measured Power
(from spec), x in px, y in px
# BeaconNumber is incremental from 0 up.  Don't skip a number
BeaconList=[]
BeaconCount = 0

Beacon = [BeaconCount,"Estimote #0 Beacon", pixelConv(314),
pixelConv(507),  "b9407f30f5f8466eaff925556b57fe6d", 64507, 5414, -64,
314, 507]
BeaconList.append(Beacon)
BeaconCount += 1
```

Finally, there is our light configuration:

```
#list of lights
#Light Format
#      LightNumber, LocalName, x, y, pixel x, pixel y, light on/off (1/0),
huelightnumber

LightList=[]
LightCount = 0
Light = [LightCount, "Lab Left", pixelConv(330), pixelConv(435),330, 435,0, 2]
LightList.append(Light)
LightCount += 1
```

You can get the Hue light number from the Phillips App under Light overview, or you can write a short program (look at the phue examples) to get the dictionary from the Phillips Hue Hub.

iBeacon Software

The iBeacons are problematic. They aren't very accurate and lots of different environmental factors affect the RSSI (received power). If you have your IOTBeaconAir sensitivities set high, you can sit in one place and watch the lights grow brighter and dimmer as the received signals vary. It's kind of a visual map of the electromagnetic spectrum. Setting your brightness sensitivities lower will increase the sensitivity, while the light range higher clears this up.

There are two functions used by IOTBeaconAir to determine position. First is the calculation of distance from RSSI. We use a smoothing function on the received RSSI values to reduce the jitter. For example:

```
def calculateDistanceWithRSSI(rssi,beaconnumber):

        beacon = conf.BeaconList[beaconnumber];
        txPower = beacon[7]
        ratio_db = txPower - rssi;
        ratio_linear = pow(10, ratio_db / 10);
        r = pow(ratio_linear, .5);
        return r
```

The result from this function is already scaled in meters.

Trilateralization

The second key piece is the calculation of position by using Trilateration. Trilateration is the method of determining the position of a point, given the distance to three control points. [citation: en.wikipedia.org/wiki/Trilateration].

⬛ **SwitchDoc Note**　When you hear someone talking about detecting where something is by measuring distance from points, they usually say "Triangulation" where they really mean "Trilateration." What is the difference? You use triangulation when you know the angle to an object from two different sources. Then you can locate the object on a plane.

In the case of iBeacons, all we know is the distance. We don't know anything about direction. We can use three distances (or iBeacons in this case) and fix the location of the Raspberry Pi on a plane. It occurs to me that we could put a directional Bluetooth antenna on a stepper motor and possibly use that to use triangulation, which means we would only need two iBeacons to find our position, rather than three as in trilateration.

The purpose of the following getXYFrom3Beacons function is to take the information from the three selected iBeacons found (a,b,c) and calculate the XY coordinates of your IOTBeaconAir device.

```
def getXYFrom3Beacons(beaconnumbera, beaconnumberb, beaconnumberc,
rollingRSSIArray):

        beacona = conf.BeaconList[beaconnumbera];
        beaconb = conf.BeaconList[beaconnumberb];
        beaconc = conf.BeaconList[beaconnumberc];
        xa = float(beacona[2])
        ya = float(beacona[3])
        xb = float(beaconb[2])
        yb = float(beaconb[3])
        xc = float(beaconc[2])
        yc = float(beaconc[3])

        ra = float(calculateDistanceWithRSSI(rollingRSSIArray[beaconnumbera],
        beaconnumbera ))
        rb = float(calculateDistanceWithRSSI(rollingRSSIArray[beaconnumberb],
        beaconnumberb ))
        rc = float(calculateDistanceWithRSSI(rollingRSSIArray[beaconnumberc],
        beaconnumberc ))

        S = (pow(xc, 2.) - pow(xb, 2.) + pow(yc, 2.) - pow(yb, 2.) +
        pow(rb, 2.) - pow(rc, 2.)) / 2.0
        T = (pow(xa, 2.) - pow(xb, 2.) + pow(ya, 2.) - pow(yb, 2.) +
        pow(rb, 2.) - pow(ra, 2.)) / 2.0

        try:
                y = ((T * (xb - xc)) - (S * (xb - xa))) / (((ya - yb) *
                (xb - xc)) - ((yc - yb) * (xb - xa)))
                x = ((y * (ya - yb)) - T) / (xb - xa)

        except ZeroDivisionError as detail:
                print 'Handling run-time error:', detail
                return [-1,-1]

        point = [x, y]
        return point
```

The IOTBeaconAir Control Panel

The IOTBeaconAir control panel is built using an app called RasPiConnect (www.milocreek.com). It allows me to build elaborate control panels on iPhones and iPads with almost no coding and especially no coding at all on the iPad/iPhone. The response is good, especially on a local network, and I get a lot of fun and colorful buttons and controls to use. I have used this app on four projects now and I'm getting quite good at using it.

The completed control panel is shown in Figure 4-8.

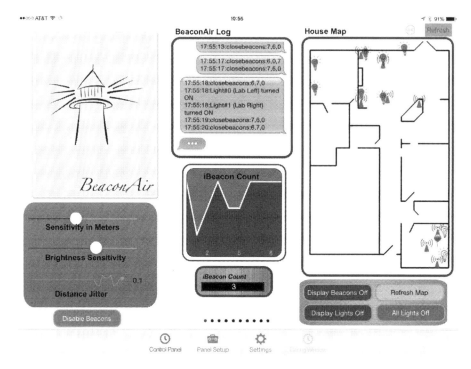

Figure 4-8. *RasPiConnect Control Screen for IOTBeaconAir*

The right side of the control panel has to do with the HTML map and control of the lights. The Remote Webview HTML control has already been discussed. The Green logging box is a Bubble Talk control and can be set up to read periodically from the server and write out logging information to the control panel. The code is contained in bubblelog.py in the IOTBeaconAir directory. In the above example you can see the close beacons drifting slightly, changing the ranking of which beacon is closest. Finally we see that two lights are turned on (you can see the results in the house map). Below that is a graph, showing how many beacons are being read. The above graph could happen if you walked out of range of the beacons and then walked back into the range.

The controls on the left side are used to set the distance in meters for which to turn the lights on for and the second control sets the brightness of the light. For example, you can set the brightness sensitivity to 1 meter and it will start getting bright at 1 meter and grow brighter as you get closer. It would be easy to modify the software to change the colors of the Phillips Hue bulbs according to distance or time of day. The graph on the bottom of the right side is a Dynamic SparkLine control set to advance every time (event driven) there is a change to the jitter value. You could also set it to a timed event, which means it advances all the time and just adds new values as they come in from IOTBeaconAir.

The code for all of the buttons is quite similar. Pushing a button on the iPad sends an HTML XML packet to the Raspberry Pi software, which then writes to a command file, which IOTBeaconAir then picks up and executes the requested functions.

In RasPiConnectServer (Local.py file) the block of code for the "All Lights On" button (a Feedback Button – FB-2) is the following:

```
# FB-2 -  turns lights on and off
 if (objectServerID == "FB-2"):
        #check for validate request
        # validate allows RasPiConnect to verify this object is here
        if (validate == "YES"):
                outgoingXMLData += Validate.buildValidateResponse("YES")
                outgoingXMLData += BuildResponse.buildFooter()
                return outgoingXMLData

        # not validate request, so execute

        responseData = "XXX"

        if (objectName is None):
                objectName = "XXX"

        lowername = objectName.lower()

        if (lowername == "all lights on"):

                status = sendCommandToBeaconAirAndWait("ALLLIGHTSON")
                responseData = "all lights off"
                responseData = responseData.title()

        elif (lowername == "all lights off"):

                status = sendCommandToBeaconAirAndWait("ALLLIGHTSOFF")
                responseData = "all lights on"
                responseData = responseData.title()

         # defaults to on
        else:
                status = sendCommandToBeaconAirAndWait("ALLLIGHTSON")
                lowername = "all lights off"
                responseData = lowername.title()

        outgoingXMLData += BuildResponse.buildResponse(responseData)
        outgoingXMLData += BuildResponse.buildFooter()
        return outgoingXMLData
```

When the button value comes ("all lights off"), the code compares it, sends a command to IOTBeaconAir, and then toggles the value ("all lights on") and sends it back to the RasPiConnect App setting up the next button push (which will next turn all the lights on). The rest of the code is boilerplate building the RasPiConnect XML request and handling an error condition that sometimes happens (the button goes blank).

The IOTBeaconAir code to handle the command file request is simple:

```
if (command == "ALLLIGHTSON"):
        lights.allLights(True, currentLightState )
        completeCommand()
        return True

if (command == "ALLLIGHTSOFF"):
        lights.allLights(False, currentLightState)
        completeCommand()
        return True
```

All of the controls follow the same design pattern, although the graphing controls are a bit more complicated. To follow any command through the system, figure out what the control ID you are looking for is (FB-2 in our example above), and track it through Local.py and then see what the command does in IOTBeaconAir.py. In some cases, such as the graphs, IOTBeaconAir is building the graph data, writing it to a file, and then RasPiConnectServer reads it in Local.py. The Remote Webview (the house map, W-10 is the object ID) is one of these controls that reads in a file generated by IOTBeaconAir. py (see the software in webmap.py). The RasPiConnect XML configuration file for IOTBeaconAir is on github.com/switchdoclabs.

The last thing to note is how to build the cool IOTBeaconAir background on the control panel screen. The trick is to build a JPEG or PNG file on any graphical app (such as Grafio on the iPad[tentouchapps.com/grafio/] or GIMP), add it to the iPad photo library, and then select the picture for the control panel background for the IOTBeaconAir page in RaspiConnect. This gives you an instant professional-looking background.

Installing blueZ and phue on the Raspberry Pi

Now it's time to install blueZ and phue on the Pi. Be prepared. The installs will take a while, too, especially the install of bluez. You can use the standard apt-get version of blueZ, but the standard apt-get version is old and has patchy support for iBeacons. Instead of using apt-get for the main blueZ package, we are downloading the source and compiling it on the Raspberry Pi. All the commands for doing this are included in the following steps. It is still a very good apt-get for the auxiliary package, which installs as shown below.

BlueZ

To install blueZ on a Raspberry Pi 3 or an older version of the Pi running the new Jessie distribution or newer distribution, run the following commands in a terminal window:

```
sudo apt-get update && sudo apt-get upgrade

sudo apt-get install libusb-dev
sudo apt-get install libglib2.0-dev --fix-missing
sudo apt-get install libudev-dev
sudo apt-get install libical-dev
sudo apt-get install libreadline-dev
sudo apt-get install libdbus-glib-1-dev

sudo apt-get install bluetooth bluez blueman

sudo apt-get install python-bluez
sudo shutdown -r now
```

To install a new version of blueZ on the Pi on older versions of the Raspberry Pi (RPi2 and before the Raspian Jessie distribution), do the following:

```
sudo apt-get install libusb-dev
sudo apt-get install libdbus-1-dev
sudo apt-get install libglib2.0-dev --fix-missing
sudo apt-get install libudev-dev
sudo apt-get install libical-dev
sudo apt-get install libreadline-dev

sudo mkdir bluez
cd bluez
sudo wget www.kernel.org/pub/linux/bluetooth/bluez-5.19.tar.gz
sudo gunzip bluez-5.19.tar.gz
sudo tar xvf bluez-5.19.tar
cd bluez-5.19
sudo ./configure --disable-systemd
sudo make
sudo make install

sudo apt-get install python-bluez

sudo shutdown -r now
```

Now you have bluez installed and running on your Raspberry Pi. Next install your USB Bluetooth 4.0 Dongle and start the checkout. For example:

```
pi@BeaconAir ~/BeaconAir/ble $ lsusb
```

```
Bus 001 Device 002: ID 0424:9512 Standard Microsystems Corp.
Bus 001 Device 001: ID 1d6b:0002 Linux Foundation 2.0 root hub
Bus 001 Device 003: ID 0424:ec00 Standard Microsystems Corp.
Bus 001 Device 004: ID 0a5c:21e8 Broadcom Corp.
```

Note, your USB Bluetooth dongle should show up something like this depending on what you have plugged into your USB bus. You can see a lot more information about the USB device by typing this:

```
sudo lsusb -v -d 0a5c:
```

Now you can look for the Bluetooth device using hciconfig:

```
pi@BeaconAir ~/BeaconAir/ble $ hciconfig
hci0: Type: BR/EDR Bus: USB
 BD Address: 00:02:72:CC:DF:D1 ACL MTU: 1021:8 SCO MTU: 64:1
 UP RUNNING
 RX bytes:9071808 acl:0 sco:0 events:230151 errors:0
 TX bytes:1166 acl:0 sco:0 commands:100 errors:0
Finally, turn on the device:
```

```
pi@BeaconAir ~/BeaconAir/ble $ sudo hciconfig hci0 up
```

And now run the blescanner (github.com/switchdoclabs/iBeacon-Scanner-) command to see what iBeacons might be around you. If you don't have an iBeacon, you can simulate it on with either your iPhone or Android phone with any number of apps on the App Store.

```
cd /home/pi/BeaconAir/ble
```

```
pi@BeaconAir ~/ble $ sudo python testblescan.py
ble thread started
----------
cf:68:cc:c7:33:10,b9407f30f5f8466eaff925556b57fe6d,13072,52423,-74,-78
cf:68:cc:c7:33:10,74696d6f74650e160a181033c7cc68cf,46608,13255,-52,-77
da:f4:2e:a0:70:b1,b9407f30f5f8466eaff925556b57fe6d,28849,11936,-74,-79
da:f4:2e:a0:70:b1,74696d6f74650e160a18b170a02ef4da,46769,28832,46,-78
dd:5d:d3:35:09:dd,8aefb0316c32486f825be26fa193487d,1,1,-64,-78
c3:11:48:9b:cf:fa,8aefb0316c32486f825be26fa193487d,0,0,-64,-73
fd:5b:12:7f:02:e4,b9407f30f5f8466eaff925556b57fe6d,740,4735,-74,-79
fd:5b:12:7f:02:e4,74696d6f74650e160a18e4027f125bfd,46820,639,18,-80
dd:5d:d3:35:09:dd,8aefb0316c32486f825be26fa193487d,1,1,-64,-77
```

The content of each line above is this:

```
example: cf:68:cc:c7:33:10,b9407f30f5f8466eaff925556b57fe6d,
13072,52423,-74,-78
Beacon MAC Address,iBeacon UDID, iBeacon Major Number, iBeacon Minor Number,
TX Power at 1m, RSSI
```

Note that there are some odd devices above that are NOT my Estimote (b9407f30f5f8466eaff925556b57fe6d) or Particle (8aefb0316c32486f825be26fa193487d) iBeacons. The txPower for the Estimote and Particle devices behave correctly. The odd devices have larger numbers or actually numbers that vary. Interesting information.

phue

The installation of phue on your Pi is simple. One approach is to execute the so-called easy install. For example:

```
sudo easy_install phue
```

The alternative is to invoke pip as follows:

```
sudo pip install phue
```

Note that after the first time you run IOTBeaconAir on your Raspberry Pi, the phue library will quit telling you that you need to push the Phillips Hue Hub button and rerun the software. IOTBeaconAir will then be paired with the Phillips Hue Hub.

RasPiConnectServer Startup

Now that all the code has been installed for iBeaconIOT, you need to start up the code. The startup procedure steps follow.

Startup Procedure

To start up IOTBeaconAir, you need to do three things.

1. Turn on the Bluetooth dongle as follows:

    sudo hciconfig hci0 up

2. Change to the IOTBeaconAir directory. Start up the
    IOTBeaconAir python programming by invoking either

    sudo python IOTBeaconAir.py (in its own terminal window)

    or

    sudo nohup python IOTBeaconAir.py & (from the command line)

3. Change to the RasPiConnectServer directory. Start the
    RasPiConnectServer. You can execute either this command:

    sudo sh startserver.sh (in its own terminal window)

    or this one:

    sudo nohup sh startserver.sh & (from the command line)

If you use nohup, you can close the terminal window and the program keeps running in the background until you reboot or kill the program. All of the debug data goes into a file nohup.out in the start directory. If you want to watch what is going on using nohup, go to the program directory and type *tail -f nohup.out* on the command line.

Making IOTBeaconAir Start on Bootup

You can make IOTBeaconAir start when the Pi boots by editing /etc/rc.local. The /etc/rc.local script is a script on the Raspberry Pi that runs when Linux first boots. To edit it, you will need root privileges. Invoking the editor via sudo is the way to go here:

sudo nano /etc/rc.local

Then add the following lines to the rc.local file. Place the newly added lines before the exit 0 statement.

sudo hciconfig hci0 up

date >> /var/log/RasPiConnectServer.log
echo "Starting RasPiConnectServer…" >> /var/log/RasPiConnectServer.log
nohup /home/pi/RasPiConnectServer/startserver.sh >>/var/log/
RasPiConnectServer.log 2>&1 &

date >> /var/log/BeaconAir.log
echo "Starting IOTBeaconAir.." >> /var/log/BeaconAir.log
cd /home/pi/BeaconAir/
nohup sudo python IOTBeaconAir.py >>/var/log/RasPiConnectServer.log 2>&1 &

How It Works in Practice

IOTBeaconAir does work. As I walk around with the IOTBeaconAir Portable Pi in a fanny pack, the lights come on and off. I have published a video of the action on www.switchdoc.com.

However, the iBeacons are not very reliable and will vary significantly just sitting in one spot. You can watch the little red pin bounce around on the control panel. A lot could be done to smooth this out by doing a little signal processing at the cost of response time. It certainly makes an interesting demo to show people.

Things to Do

You can use the MQTT techniques of Chapters 5 and 6 to connect the IOTBeaconAir to an external IOT Server or tweet your location as in Chapter 3.

One idea I had for another project revolving around iBeacons was to reverse the system. Carry an iBeacon and build a mesh network of Raspberry Pi's all listening to the iBeacon via my BLE scanner program and then communicating the RSSI information to a central Pi that would figure out the location of the iBeacon and report it to the control panel. Now granted, it's more expensive than buying a bunch of iBeacons and one Pi, but it would have some really interesting data flows and the response time could be excellent. It would be a lot better for the user as she would just have to carry a small iBeacon in her pocket! Better for the fashion conscious than a fanny pack. Figure 4-9 shows IOTBeaconAir installed in a very fashion-conscious fanny pack.

Figure 4-9. *IOTBeaconAir Ready to Walk*

The first thing I would add to this unit is the ability for the Raspberry Pi to sense the light levels in the environment. Why turn the lights on if it is already bright in the room?

The Classic Distributed System Problems

Now I will talk about the classic problem with groups of IOT devices. What do you do if two IOT units are telling your lights two different things? Who wins?

If we were to build a bunch of these devices and put them on other members of the household (other people or the cat), we now need to build an arbitration system. What do I mean by that? We have to "arbitrate" the information coming in from the IOT devices. In computer speak, a group of IOTBeaconAir units with no central coordinator becomes a distributed system. From the Wikipedia definition of distributed systems [en.wikipedia. org/wiki/Distributed_computing], "A distributed system is a software system in which components located on networked computers communicate and coordinate their actions by passing messages. The components interact with each other in order to achieve a common goal. Three significant characteristics of distributed systems are: concurrency of components, lack of a global clock, and independent failure of components." You can see from this that any group of IOT devices fit within this definition.

Since there is no global server for IOTBeaconAir, there is no mechanism currently defined to handle arbitration of actions based on detection. In general, it is easier to resolve these kinds of issues by using a global server. But, this makes your system more susceptible to failure of the server. Group self-organization and group arbitration is a better way to go, but it is much more complicated to design, implement, and test.

Here are some of the questions to arbitrate once you have multiple IOT units of IOTBeaconAir:

- Which IOTBeaconAir turns the lights on?

- Which IOTBeaconAir turns the lights off?

- How do you handle one person leaving the room?

- How do you rank the IOTBeaconAir units to one another? Is the cat on the bottom or top of the priority list?

- How do you handle people turning lights on or off by hand?

- How do you detect a person sitting down to read versus walking through the house?

And the list goes on. Any time you put more than one IOT device in control of anything physical at all, things can get very complicated.

Conclusion

In Chapter 3, we built an IOT Weather device that generated and supplied information to the rest of the Internet. In this chapter you saw how IOTBeaconAir reverses that. It gathers information from the IOT devices (iBeacons) around itself, and then modifies the environment without going out to the Internet (or the wider IOT) at all. This is a much more localized IOT application.

In Chapter 6, we'll extend this idea further by building an RFID (Radio Frequency IDentification) unit that will gather information from passive units (that are only activated when they are being interrogated for information) and then do both major functions. Send data to the Internet and modify the local environment.

For all of the software, see the following:

`github/switchdoclabs/BeaconAirPython`

`github/switchdoclabs/BeaconAirRasPiConnectLocal`

`github/switchdoclabs/iBeacon-Scanner-`

For more on IOTBeaconAir and discussion: `www.switchdoc.com`

CHAPTER 5

■ ■ ■

Connecting an IOT Device to a Cloud Server - IOTPulse

Chapter Goal: Build a Portable IOT Device for Reading Your Pulse

Topics Covered in This Chapter:

- IOT on a Global Network

- Bluemix and the Internet Of Things

- The IOTPulse Design

- Building the IOTPulse Device

- Connecting and testing the hardware and software for IOTPulse

- Setting up IBM Bluemix and Connecting IOTPulse

- Examining Results and Advanced Features

This chapter will show the reader how to connect an IOT device to a cloud server, IBM Bluemix. The complexity in this chapter is not building the device, but rather navigating the setup process for adding your device to the cloud.

A major part of designing devices that will connect with the IOT is to determine what to do with the data after you have gathered it. A huge amount of data and no way to store it or analyze it is not very useful. An IOT project device generally is very CPU limited and also only has a limited amount of storage available. You generally have to send the data collected by a sensor-filled IOT device up to a bigger computer and storage cloud to perform complex analysis and determine actions on that data.

In this chapter, we are building a device to collect the pulse rate from a person, and then periodically (every 10 seconds) send it up to a cloud-based storage and analysis system called the IBM Bluemix IOT Foundation.

Before we selected the IBM Bluemix for this chapter, we also looked at three other providers. We determined that the Amazon IOT solution was too "heavy" for these small devices because of the protocol and encryption required. The two other smaller vendors were rejected because of length of time in existence and limited analysis functionality. It should be pointed out that the smaller vendors had distinctly superior display capabilities out of the box from either of the two majors.

© John C. Shovic 2016
J. C. Shovic, *Raspberry Pi IoT Projects*, DOI 10.1007/978-1-4842-1377-3_5

The IBM Bluemix system brought a good mix of flexible protocols, a "light" method for sending data, and an amazing collection of analytical tools. Ramifications of the IBM Bluemix methodology on encryption versus the Amazon IOT solution will be discussed in Chapter 7, "Computer Security and the IOT."

IOT Characterization of This Project

As we discussed in Chapter 1, the first thing to do to understand an IOT project is to look at our six different aspects of IOT shown in Table 5-1. IOTPulse is a more complex project than LightSwarm and is much closer to a production IOT device.

Table 5-1. IOTPulse Characterization (CPLPFC)

Aspect	Rating	Comments
Communications	9	WiFi connection to Internet -
Processor Power	7	80MHz XTensa Harvard Architecture CPU, ~80KB Data RAM / ~35KB of Instruction RAM / 200K ROM
Local Storage	8	4MB Flash (or 3MB file system!)
Power Consumption	8	~200mA transmitting, ~60mA receiving, noWiFi ~15mA, Standby ~1mA
Functionality	7	Partial Arduino Support (limited GPIO/Analog Inputs)
Cost	9	< $10 and getting cheaper

Ratings are from 1–10, 1 being the least suitable for IOT and 10 being the most suitable for IOT applications.

This gives us a CPLPFC rating of 8.0. Great for learning and experimenting, and it could be deployed for some market applications.

The ESP8266 provides a WiFi transmitter/receiver, a TCP/IP stack, and firmware to support direction connections to a local WiFi access point, which then can connect to the Internet. The data generated by the IOTPulse design will be sent to IBM's Bluemix Cloud IOT site.

The Internet Of Things on the Global Network

As was stated in the introduction, what do you do with all this data you are gathering? Whether it is the age of your milk in the refrigerator, your current blood sugar or pulse rate, or your home security system, the data needs to be stored and analyzed; or what is the point of gathering it?

Sometimes you don't need to store the data. Sometimes the local devices can do the necessary actions (like in the LightSwarm project in Chapter 2), but there are many applications that require more computing resources than might be available among the local IOT devices.

This is the situation that has led to the development of server-based (often on a computing cloud) support software for the upcoming IOT explosion. In Chapter 2, we used a Raspberry Pi to gather the data from the LightSwarm and log the rather complex behavior of the cooperative swarm itself for later analysis. If you have a thousand devices, you most likely are not going to be able to host your server on a Raspberry Pi, which has limited CPU power and storage. Another major problem with basing your system on physical servers that you control (like Raspberry Pis, but also rack mount servers with much larger CPU and memory capabilities) is that of scalability. If suddenly you have 10,000 devices connecting to your servers instead of 1,000 devices, you need to be able to scale quickly and effectively.

It is this realization that IOT systems need to scale quickly and efficiently that has moved the IOT back-end applications into the realm of cloud computing. For an IOT application, there are three main areas that need to be addressed. They are the following: Cloud Computing, Application Builders, and Report and Generation software.

Cloud Computing

Cloud computing is evolving quickly to morph into more services, ubiquitous back ends, high-speed network connectivity, and multiple languages and solutions. The National Institute of Science and Technology (NIST) provides a document that defines cloud computing for government purposes [http://csrc.nist.gov/publications/nistpubs/800-145/SP800-145.pdf]. While parts of it are already outdated, it does give a good base definition of cloud computing.

NIST defines cloud computing as this: "Cloud computing is a model for enabling ubiquitous, convenient, on-demand network access to a shared pool of configurable computing resources (e.g., networks, servers, storage, applications, and services) that can be rapidly provisioned and released with minimal management effort or service provider interaction."

The essential characteristics of cloud computing are the following:

1. On-Demand - User can provision computing services as needed without requiring interaction with service provider.

2. High Internet Connectivity - Cloud capabilities are available over the network and accessed through mechanisms that promote multiple platform usage (not just desktops, but many other types of computers and devices).

3. Ability to Pool Resources - Resources such as memory, CPU power, and storage are pooled to support multiple users and customers according to user demand.

4. Rapid Scaling - Capabilities and resources can be provisioned and released automatically or under user control. With the proper system and software, the cloud can look to be virtually unlimited to the user or application.

5.   Ability to Limit (or Meter) Resources - A cloud will be able to limit resources and optimize resource use at several levels of abstraction.

6.   Ability to Charge for Service - A cloud service is able to account for resource usage, be able to monitor those resources, and report usage in a transparent manner for both the supplier and the user of the system.

Application Builders

There is no way that a cloud provider can anticipate every application or use for data that an IOT provider will need. A good cloud provider will support major types of databases and a variety of standard software Application Programming Interfaces (APIs). It will provide analytical tools for the data and a variety of different services for manipulating that data. A cloud application (or cloud app) is a program that runs in a cloud environment. It has some aspects of a pure local app (for an iPad or a desktop) and some aspects of a pure web-based app. A local app will reside entirely on your local computer, while a web app is generally stored entirely on a remote computer and is delivered via a browser interface. There are web apps that are a hybrid (such as WebEx) that have a very light client on the browser side (still an app, but a small one) that connects up via an API to a much more complex program on the server side. The application builders in IBM Bluemix have a heavier client (running the graphics and editing part of the application) and then deliver the user design to the servers via an API.

In the IOT world, an application often has both aspects, where the local computer contains part of the application (say sensor data gathering) and the cloud contains the back-end heavy metal processing for the full application. The IOTPulse project is one of these mixed types of applications.

Display and Report Generation

Displaying pertinent information to the user about the user's IOT devices and what actions they are performing on the user's behalf is an important aspect that will lead to the adoption of widespread IOT applications. It is argued by some that it is important not to overwhelm the user with data about what is going on. However, we believe that the "overwhelming" part of the IOT can be handled with hierarchical interfaces. The top-most level of the user interface may only display the very basic information needed by the user (say temperature and furnace status). The author attended an early meeting on what was to become the IOT at Microsoft in Redmond, Washington, and the speaker called the most basic mode "Grandma Mode" because he felt there was a need to support substantially every type of user that was going to be using the product with a simple interface.

We felt this was true as far as it went, but with the IOT, the ability for a device and software interface to show what is going on with the data being gathered is paramount. A method and interface needs to be provided for the user to really drill down and look at what is happening inside his network and device at several different levels. Not as part of the "Grandma Mode" interface, but another set of interfaces that are accessible to any user if the user should wish.

Doing this hierarchical interface is a key part of establishing the necessary trust between the user and the IOT device.

A well-designed cloud-based application and report generation system needs to provide the application developer many different ways of analyzing the data, acting on the data, and displaying the data. The cloud developer will never be able to supply all the possible build interfaces that the app developer will need for every application.

The IBM Bluemix Internet Of Things Solution

Bluemix (Figure 5-1) is an IOT-focused implementation of IBM's Open Cloud Architecture that enables you to create, deploy, and manage cloud applications for the Internet Of Things.

Figure 5-1. The IBM Bluemix Logo

There is a growing ecosystem of runtime frameworks and services, including non-IBM third-party solutions and applications. Bluemix provides a dashboard for you to create, view, and manage your applications, IOT devices, and desired services The Bluemix dashboards also provide the ability to manage organizations, spaces, and (very importantly!) user access.

We did find that the "dashboard" paradigm in the Bluemix system somewhat of a misnomer and a bit confusing. Instead of having one dashboard, you have dashboards for every service that you attach. It's easy to get lost in the sequence. But with some perseverance we got through the learning curve.

Bluemix provides access to a wide variety of services that can be incorporated into an application from multiple vendors.

151

For more complex applications than the IOTPulse device, you have a set of application libraries that you can build your applications connecting to a variety of databases functions and frameworks. Here are some of the more common ones:

- Node.js
- PHP
- Python
- Ruby

All in all, Bluemix is a good implementation of a cloud-based IOT platform to build upon.

Note that Bluemix is an evolving platform, and there will be changes going forward in their product maturation process.

There are many features that are free for prototypes (such as IOTPulse), and all of the features mentioned in this chapter are free for use on Bluemix. Looking through the paid services and rates, it seems that they are reasonable for both small and large applications.

The IOTPulse Design

The IOTPulse design consists of three blocks. The first block is the ESP8266 and the 9V battery, which contains the computer; the WiFi interface; and a single Analog to Digital Converter (ADC) pin, called A on the ESP8266 board and A0 inside the Arduino IDE software. The ESP8266 is responsible for doing the signal processing and translation of the incoming analog heartbeat signal to a digital heartbeats per minute (BPM) and then will periodically send the latest BPM up to the Bluemix IOT cloud.

The second block is the Pulse Sensor Amped, which is an open source hardware design by `www.pulsesensor.com`. Figure 5-2 shows the schematic for the Pulse Sensor. The key thing to take away from the pulse sensor is that it is designed to get an approximate measure of heart rate through the skin in a non-invasive way. It works by shining a bright green LED into your skin and then detecting the relative changes in light intensity to the sensor. With a small amount of signal shaping, you can detect pulse rate via an analog output signal.

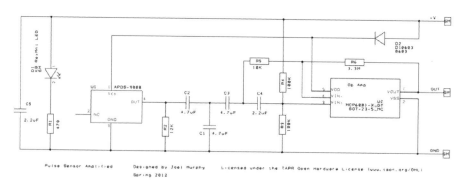

Figure 5-2. *Schematic for the Pulse Sensor*

For more information on the technique, see photoplethysmogram [`https://en.wikipedia.org/wiki/Photoplethysmogram`].

The third block is a resistor-based voltage divider. The issue that we are solving with this voltage divider is that the signal output from the Pulse Sensor is about 1.5V and the ADC input on the ESP8266 only goes up to 1V. For a full description on how a voltage divider works, check out the Wikipedia article [`https://en.wikipedia.org/wiki/Voltage_divider`].

We need to take 1.5V down to about 0.6V for the ESP8266 and the software to work. The Pulse Sensor provides a signal that on the average is about 1.5V, which is too high for the ESP8266 ADC to work correctly. With the choice of a 26K Ohm resistor for R1 in Figure 5-3 and an 18K Ohm resistor for R2 in Figure 5-3, we get the following ratio of input to output voltage:

```
Vout = Vin * R2/(R1 + R2)
```

```
Vout = 1.5V * 18K/(26K + 18K) = 0.6V
```

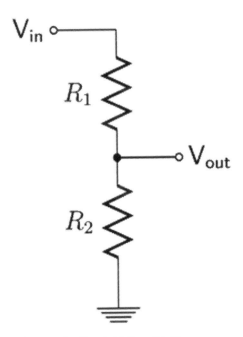

Figure 5-3. *Simple Voltage Divider*

The 0.6V is comfortably in the 0.0 - 1.0V range of the ESP8266 ADC and works well. There is virtually no current drain through this voltage divider because of the high resistance of the voltage divider (44K Ohms).

Why does this work? It is because the software in the ESP8266 is calculating the heartbeat by looking at relative changes in the light intensity and not the absolute voltage. As long as the input value is changing, the ESP8266 will pick up the pulse.

If we did not put the voltage divider on the output of the Pulse Sensor, then the ADC in the ESP8266 would always be pegged to the highest level (1.0V) and the sensor software would not be able to pick up a pulse.

Because the ESP8266 ADC is so limited, there are better solutions out there for an ADC. Two of the easier to use boards are these:

- Seeedstudio Grove I2C ADC – 1 channel, 12 bits (requires 5V – needs some help to work with the ESP8266) [www.seeedstudio.com/wiki/Grove_-_I2C_ADC]

- SwitchDoc Labs Grove I2C ADC – 4 channels, 16 bits 3.3V/5V compatible [www.switchdoc.com/grove-4-channel-16-bit-adc-based-ads1115/]

Figure 5-4 shows the block diagram, including the voltage divider, of the IOTPulse project. The completed IOTPulse device, including the 3D Printed case is shown in Figure 5-5.

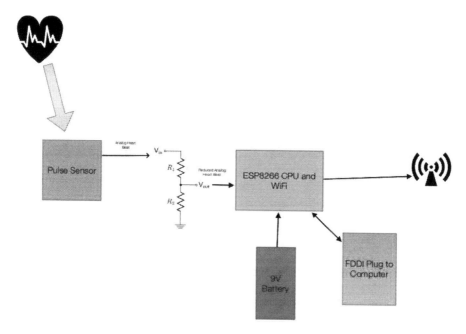

Figure 5-4. *Block Diagram of IOTPulse*

154

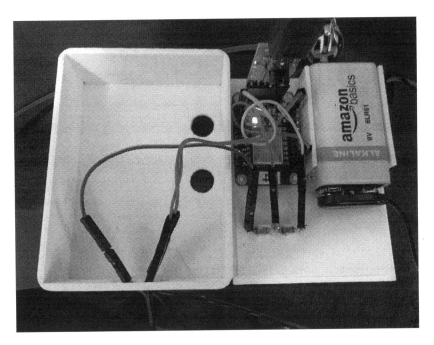

Figure 5-5. *IOTPulse in Case*

Building the IOTPulse

The parts list is shown in Table 5-2, followed by the wiring list. The parts for the IOTPulse device are readily available and only the voltage divider will require any soldering.

Table 5-2. *Parts List*

Part Number	Count	Description	Approximate Cost per Board	Source
ESP8266 Huzzah Board	1	CPU / WiFi board	$10	`http://www.adafruit.com/products/2471`
Pulse Sensor Amped	1	I2C Light Sensor	$25	`www.Pulsesensor.com`
FTDI Cable	1	Cable for programming the ESP8266 from PC/Mac	$11	`http://www.switchdoc.com/inexpensive-ftdi-cable-for-arduino-esp8266-includes-usb-cable/`

(continued)

Table 5-2. (continued)

Part Number	Count	Description	Approximate Cost per Board	Source
26K Ohm Resistor	1	1/4 watt	$17 for a large mix of resistors (Joe Knows Electronics)	http://amzn. to/1QCASLB
18K Ohm Resistor	1	1/4 watt	$17 for a large mix of resistors (Joe Knows Electronics)	http://amzn. to/1QCASLB

Plugging the FTDI Cable into the ESP8266

An FTDI cable is plugged into the end of the Adafruit Huzzah ESP8266. Make sure you align the GND pin on the FTDI Cable with the GND pin on the ESP8266 breakout board as shown in Figure 5-6.

Figure 5-6. FTDI Cable Plugged into the Huzzah Board. Note GND Connection

Table 5-3 contains the wiring list for the IOTPulse project.

Table 5-3. *IOTPulse Wiring List*

From	To	Description
ESP8266/GND	PulseSensor / GND (Black Wire)	Ground for Pulse Sensor
ESP8266/3V	PulseSensor / 3.3V (Red Wire)	3.3V Power for Pulse Sensor
PulseSensor/Output (Purple Wire)	26K / Port A	Top of the Resistor Divider
26K/Port B	18K / Port A	Middle of the Resistor Divider
18K/Port A	ESP8266 / GND	Ground for bottom of Resistor Divider
26K/Port B	ESP8266 / A0	A0 - Analog to Digital Converter input on ESP8266

3D Printing Files for the IOT Case

Finding a case for a custom project can always be a problem. All of the projects in the chapters have suggested using 3D Printing to build cases that fit the project, and the IOTPulse project is no different. The most interesting part of this case is the way we designed a bevel that goes around the base so the top case will snap onto the bottom case (Figure 5-7).

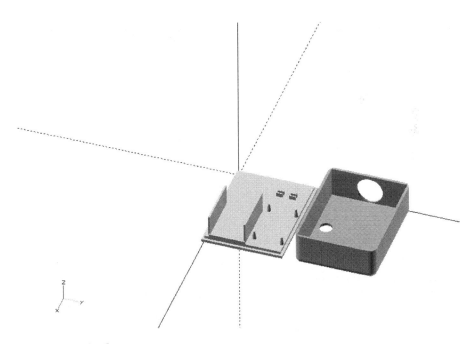

Figure 5-7. *IOT Case*

We have introduced openSCAD, a free code-based 3D Modeler in previous chapters. There are hundreds of example models on Thingverse.com and the openSCAD web site to choose from and to learn from. Listing 5-1 contains the code that builds the case shown in Figure 5-7.

Listing 5-1. openSCAD code for the IOT Case

```
//
// IOTPulse Case
//
// SwitchDoc Labs
// August 2015
//

include <RoundedRect.scad>

module rcube(size=[30, 20, 10], radius=[3, 2, 1], center=true)
    hull() {
        translate( center ? [0,0,0] : size/2 ) {
            cube(size-2*radius+[2*radius[0],0,0],center=true);
            cube(size-2*radius+[0,2*radius[1],0],center=true);
            cube(size-2*radius+[0,0,2*radius[2]],center=true);

            for(x = [-0.5,0.5], y = [-0.5,0.5], z = [-0.5,0.5])
                translate([x * ( size[0] - 2*radius[0]),
                           y * ( size[1] - 2*radius[1]),
                           z * ( size[2] - 2*radius[2])])
                    scale([radius[0], radius[1], radius[2]])
//                      sphere(1.0,$fn=4*4);
                        sphere(1.0,$fn=6*6);
        }
    }

module IOTPulseTopCase()
{

    difference()
    {
        //cube([82,62,25]);

        rcube(size=[82,62,30],radius=[5,5,5],center=false);

        #translate([2,2,2])
        cube([78,58,25]);

        #translate([-10,-10,25])
        cube( [100,100,50]);

        // hole for pulse meter 18mm
```

```
        translate([-5,62/2,12.5])
        #rotate([0,90,0])
        cylinder(h=10,r=10,10);

        // hole for seeing light
        #translate([82-20,10,-2])
        cylinder(h=10,r=5,10);

        // hole for seeing wifi light
        #translate([82-43,10,-2])
        cylinder(h=10,r=5,10);

    }

}

union()
{

    cube([78,58,4]);
    translate([-2,-2,0])
    cube([82,62,2]);

    // Mount for Battery

    translate([40-2,2,0])
    cube([40-2,1.35,20]);
    translate([40-2,26.10+3.3,0])
    cube([40-2,1.5,20]);

    // lips for battery
    translate([79-2,3,0])
    cube([1,28,6]);

    // plyons for ESP8266

    translate([70-1.0,35,0])
    cylinder(h=10,r1=2.2, r2=1.35/2, $fn=100);
    translate([70-1.0,56,0])
    cylinder(h=10,r1=2.2, r2=1.35/2, $fn=100);
    translate([70-34,35,0])
    cylinder(h=10,r1=2.2, r2=1.35/2, $fn=100);
    translate([70-34,56,0])
    cylinder(h=10,r1=2.2, r2=1.35/2, $fn=100);

    // plyons for resistors for divider

    // gap of 2.3mm
```

```
    translate([15,35,2])
    cube([1,5,5]);

    translate([15+3,35,2])
    cube([1,5,5]);

   translate([15,45,2])
    cube([1,5,5]);

    translate([15+3,45,2])
    cube([1,5,5]);

   // top case

    translate([0,70,0])
    IOTPulseTopCase();
}
```

The code for the IOTPulse case is broken into two main sections. The main program builds the lower part of the case while the top of the case is located in the function IOTPulseTopCase(). When building models with openSCAD, it is a good idea to break different parts into functions even if you are only calling them once. It simplifies the code. Now, let us look at the software for IOTPulse.

Software Needed

For you to program the IOT Pulse board you will need a Mac or PC to program the ESP8266 via the Arduino IDE. See Chapter 2 for how to set up the Arduino IDE with the ESP8266 libraries.

The IOTPulse Code

There are three files that are part of the build for the IOTPulse software. The IOTPulse.ino is the main Arduino IDE file (in the C language), and the other two files (Interrupt.h and AllSerialHandling.h) are included in the main file. While the code is fairly straightforward, comments need to be made for each module.

IOTPulse.ino

IOTPulse.ino is the main program for IOTPulse (Listing 5-2). It consists of two major functions, setup() and loop(). The setup() function initializes the ESP8266 WiFi code, reads an IP address using DCHP from the local wireless access point, and initializes variables for containing micros(), which is a function returning the number of microseconds since the reboot of the ESP8266 micros() is a timekeeping function. Note that the ESP8266 does not have a real-time clock on board and really doesn't know what time it is. It only knows how long it has been running. If you wish to set the time of day in the ESP8266, please check out the NTP protocol in this Instructable[http://www.instructables.com/id/Internet-time-syncronized-clock-for-Arduino/].

In the IOTPulse project, we really don't care what time it is. When we send a sample to the Bluemix IOT Platform, our friend IBM will timestamp the reception of the data. If we cared about our time, we could build an NTP receiver and synchronize it to network time at a specific NTP server. We are much more interested in intervals of time (specifically 2 milliseconds and 10 seconds intervals) rather than absolute time.

The loop() function contains the code for ongoing operation of the IOTPulse data-gathering operation. We basically do four things in the loop() function:

- We check the value of QS. If QS is true, then the software in Interrupt.h has found a BPM (Beats Per Minute) and IBI (Interval Between beats) value for the current pulse rate for our PulseSensor connected to your ear.

- Next, if 10 seconds have elapsed (10,000,000 microseconds), we send the current value of BPM and IBI up to the IBM Bluemix IOT cloud. We then reset the time to wait for the next 10-second interval, which is stored in the oldIOTTime variable. The actual time for the next interval is oldIOTTime + 10 seconds (10,000,000 microseconds).

- If 2 milliseconds have elapsed since oldPulseTime variable (initialized in loop()), we call the timerCallback() function defined in Interrupt.h. We then reset the oldPulseTime variable and wait for another 2ms.

Note at the end of the loop() function, there is a yield() function. This MUST be called periodically for the ESP8266 software to continue running the WiFi interface and other housekeeping functions. Remember, unlike a regular Arduino, there is a great deal going on in the background to keep this chip running and connected to the network.

One limitation of the current ESP8266 software is that you can't use the timers [http://www.switchdoc.com/2015/10/iot-esp8266-timer-tutorial-arduino-ide/] to generate interrupts without causing the WiFi to fail and stop connecting to the local WiFi access point and the Internet.

This makes it very difficult to generate an interrupt to the computer every 2ms as is called for by the PulseSensor. You could generate an interrupt every 2ms by using an external hardware timer and then connecting the output of the hardware timer to one of the GPIO pins on the ESP8266, which can all be programmed to generate an interrupt to the CPU.

To solve this issue, we use a scheduling technique that is more CPU intensive (read uses more power) than the interrupt scheme. We check the time periodically and run the PulseSensor software every 2ms and also connect to the IBM Bluemix every 10 seconds.

The biggest disadvantage of this is that we cannot "sleep" the processor very easily. We are looking for an alternative architecture for this problem and are watching the ESP8266 development web sites for solutions.

However, with the exception of power consumption, the current solution works well.

Listing 5-2. IOTPulse.ino

```
/*

    SwitchDoc Labs Code for IOT Pulse
    Connects Pulse detector to the IBM Bluemix IoT using a ESP8266 processor
    based on pulsecounting code from www.pulsesensor.com
    November 2015


    --------------------- Notes --------------------- ---------------------
    This code:
    1) Blinks an LED to User's Live Heartbeat   PIN 0

    2) Determines BPM

    3) Sends information to the IBM Bluemix IOT
*/

extern "C" {
#include "user_interface.h"
}
#include <ESP8266WiFi.h>
#include <PubSubClient.h> // https://github.com/knolleary/pubsubclient/
releases/tag/v2.3


//-----------------------------------------------------------------------
//Local WiFi Variables

const char* ssid = "yourssid";
const char* password = "yourpassword";

#define IOTPULSEVERSION 004

// IBM BlueMix IOT Foundation Data

#define ORG "XXXXX"
#define DEVICE_TYPE "IOTPulse-01"
#define DEVICE_ID "1"
#define TOKEN "YYYYYYYYY"

// setup for IOT IBM

char server[] = ORG ".messaging.internetofthings.ibmcloud.com";
char topic[] = "iot-2/evt/status/fmt/json";
char authMethod[] = "use-token-auth";
char token[] = TOKEN;
char clientId[] = "d:" ORG ":" DEVICE_TYPE ":" DEVICE_ID;
```

```
//-----------------------------------------------------------------------

//  Variables
int pulsePin = A0;                      // Pulse Sensor purple wire connected to
                                        analog pin 0
int blinkPin = 0;                       // pin to blink led at each beat
int fadePin = 5;                        // pin to do fancy classy fading blink
                                        at each beat
int fadeRate = 0;                       // used to fade LED on with PWM on fadePin

// Volatile Variables, used in the interrupt service routine!
volatile int BPM;                       // int that holds raw Analog in 0.
                                        updated every 2mS
volatile int Signal;                    // holds the incoming raw data
volatile int IBI = 600;                 // int that holds the time interval
                                        between beats! Must be seeded!
volatile boolean Pulse = false;         // "True" when User's live heartbeat is
                                        detected. "False" when not a "live beat".
volatile boolean QS = false;            // becomes true when Arduoino finds a beat.

// Regards Serial OutPut  -- Set This Up to your needs
static boolean serialData = true;       // Set to 'false' by Default.  Re-set to
                                        'true' to see Arduino Serial Monitor data

#include "AllSerialHandling.h"
#include "Interrupt.h"

void callback(char* topic, byte* payload, unsigned int length) {
  Serial.println("callback invoked from IOT BlueMix");
}

WiFiClient wifiClient;
PubSubClient client(server, 1883, callback, wifiClient);

unsigned long oldPulseTime;
unsigned long oldIOTTime;

void setup() {

  pinMode(blinkPin, OUTPUT);            // pin that will blink to your heartbeat!

  Serial.begin(115200);                 // we agree to talk fast!

  Serial.println("----------------");
  Serial.println("IOTPulse IBM Bluemix IOT");
  Serial.println("----------------");
```

```
Serial.print("Connecting to ");
Serial.print(ssid);

// NOTE below:  Newer versions of the ESP8266 Libraries may require the
following statement
// instead of the other statement.  WiFi.SSID() has changed definitions in
new versions
// if (strcmp (WiFi.SSID().c_str(), ssid) != 0) {

if (strcmp (WiFi.SSID(), ssid) != 0) {
  WiFi.begin(ssid, password);
}
while (WiFi.status() != WL_CONNECTED) {
  delay(500);
  Serial.print(".");
}
Serial.println("");

Serial.print("Local WiFi connected, IP address: ");
Serial.println(WiFi.localIP());

// interruptSetup();                    // sets up to read Pulse Sensor
                                        signal every 2mS
// Note:  Interrupts based on os_timer seems to break the ESP8266
WiFi.  Moving to micros() polling methodology
oldPulseTime = micros();
oldIOTTime = micros();
}

int sampleCount = 0;
int beatCount = 0;

int beatValue = 0;
unsigned long newPulseDeltaTime;
unsigned long newIOTDeltaTime;

//  Where the Magic Happens
void loop() {

  //serialOutput() ;

  if (QS == true) {       // A Heartbeat Was Found
    // BPM and IBI have been Determined
    // Quantified Self "QS" true when arduino finds a heartbeat
    digitalWrite(blinkPin, LOW);     // Blink LED, we got a beat.
    beatCount++;
```

```
  serialOutputWhenBeatHappens();    // A Beat Happened, Output that to serial.
  QS = false;                       // reset the Quantified Self flag for
                                    // next time
}

newPulseDeltaTime = micros() - oldPulseTime; // doing this handles the 71
second rollover because of unsighned arithmetic

newIOTDeltaTime = micros() - oldIOTTime; // doing this handles the 71
second rollover because of unsighned arithmetic

// do this every ten seconds
if (newIOTDeltaTime > 10000000)  // check for 10sec work to be done
{

  Serial.print("IOT Delta time =");
  Serial.println(newIOTDeltaTime);
  sampleCount++;

  // Sending payload: {"d":{"IOTPulse":"IP1","VER":2"SC":0,"BPM":235,"IBI":252}}

  String payload = "{\"d\":{\"IOTPulse\":\"IP1\",";
  payload += "\"VER\":";
  payload += IOTPULSEVERSION;
  payload += ",\"SC\":";
  payload += sampleCount;
  payload += ",\"BPM\":";
  payload += BPM;
  payload += ",\"IBI\":";
  payload += IBI;
  payload += ",\"BC\":";
  payload += beatCount;
  payload += "}}";

  if (!!!client.connected()) {
    Serial.print("Reconnecting client to ");
    Serial.println(server);
    while (!!!client.connect(clientId, authMethod, token)) {
      Serial.print(".");
      delay(500);
    }
    Serial.println();
  }

  Serial.print("Sending IOTPulse payload: ");
  Serial.println(payload);
```

```
    if (client.publish(topic, (char*) payload.c_str())) {
      Serial.println("BlueMix IOT Publish ok");
    } else {
      Serial.println("BlueMix IOT Publish failed");
    }
    oldIOTTime = micros();

    // restart the pulse counter
    restartPulse();
  }

  //Serial.print("micros()=");
  //Serial.println(micros());

  if (newPulseDeltaTime > 2000)  // check for 2ms work to be done
  {

    //Serial.print("Pulse Delta time =");
    //Serial.println(newPulseDeltaTime);
    // do the work for pulse calculation
    timerCallback(NULL);

    oldPulseTime = micros();
  }

  yield(); //  take a break
}
```

AllserialHandling.h (Listing 5-3) contains the serial output debugging routines that
are useful when modifying the code.

Listing 5-3. AllSerialHandling.h

```
//////////
//////////  All Serial Handling Code,
//////////  It's Changeable with the 'serialVisual' variable
//////////  Set it to 'true' or 'false' when it's declared at start of code.
//////////

void sendDataToSerial(char symbol, int data );

void serialOutput() {  // Decide How To Output Serial.

    sendDataToSerial('S', Signal);     // goes to sendDataToSerial function
}

//  Decides How To OutPut BPM and IBI Data
void serialOutputWhenBeatHappens() {
```

```
  if (serialData == true) {             //  Code to Make the Serial Monitor
  Visualizer Work
    Serial.print("*** Heart-Beat Happened *** ");   //ASCII Art Madness
    Serial.print("BPM: ");
    Serial.print(BPM);
    Serial.print(" IBI: ");
    Serial.print(IBI);
    Serial.println("  ");
  }
}

//  Sends Data to Pulse Sensor Processing App, Native Mac App, or Third-
party Serial Readers.
void sendDataToSerial(char symbol, int data ) {
  Serial.print(symbol);

  Serial.println(data);
}
```

Interrupt.h (Listing 5-4) is called this because the original PulseSensor software used an Arduino timer to generate a 2ms interrupt. As is explained above, the ESP8266 is not currently capable of doing the same thing while maintaining a functional WiFi interface. The function timerCallback() in Interrupt.h is now called at a scheduled time by the loop() function in the IOTPulse.ino file.

Basically, timerCallback() acts as a detector and averaging filter that detects the upswing on the PulseSensor output and then builds a set of times for IBI (Interval Between beats) and provides an average. It adjusts to the recorded levels coming from the PulseSensor because the actual level is not as important as the time interval between adjusted pulses from the PulseSensor. The software acts as a peak and trough detector with an average system that removes high-frequency noise.

Listing 5-4. Interrupt.h

```
volatile int rate[10];                   // array to hold last ten IBI values
volatile unsigned long sampleCounter = 0;  // used to determine pulse timing
volatile unsigned long lastBeatTime = 0;   // used to find IBI
volatile int P = 680;                    // used to find peak in pulse
                                            wave, seeded 512
volatile int T = 680;                    // used to find trough in pulse
                                            wave, seeded 512
volatile int thresh = 700;               // used to find instant moment of
                                            heart beat, seeded 525
volatile int amp = 100;                  // used to hold amplitude of pulse
                                            waveform, seeded
volatile boolean firstBeat = true;       // used to seed rate array so we
                                            startup with reasonable BPM
```

```
volatile boolean secondBeat = false;       // used to seed rate array so we
                                            // startup with reasonable BPM


void restartPulse()
{

  sampleCounter = 0;           // used to determine pulse timing
  lastBeatTime = 0;            // used to find IBI
  P = 680;                     // used to find peak in pulse wave, seeded 512
  T = 680;                     // used to find trough in pulse wave, seeded 512
  thresh = 700;                // used to find instant moment of heart beat,
                               // seeded 525
  amp = 100;                   // used to hold amplitude of pulse waveform, seeded
  firstBeat = true;            // used to seed rate array so we startup with
                               // reasonable BPM

  secondBeat = false;


}
void timerCallback(void *pArg);

// Timer  makes sure that we take a reading every 2 miliseconds
void timerCallback(void *pArg) {             // triggered on interrupts
  //cli();                                    // disable interrupts while we
                                             // do this

  Signal = analogRead(pulsePin);            // read the Pulse Sensor
  //Serial.print("Signal-A0-:");
  //Serial.println(Signal);

  sampleCounter += 2;                        // keep track of the time in
                                             // mS with this variable
  int N = sampleCounter - lastBeatTime;     // monitor the time since the
                                             // last beat to avoid noise

  //  find the peak and trough of the pulse wave
  if (Signal < thresh && N > (IBI / 5) * 3) { // avoid dichrotic noise by
                                             // waiting 3/5 of last IBI
    if (Signal < T) {                        // T is the trough
      T = Signal;                            // keep track of lowest point
                                             // in pulse wave
    }
  }

  if (Signal > thresh && Signal > P) {       // thresh condition helps
                                             // avoid noise
    P = Signal;                              // P is the peak
  }                                          // keep track of highest point
                                             // in pulse wave
```

```
//  NOW IT'S TIME TO LOOK FOR THE HEART BEAT
// signal surges up in value every time there is a pulse
if (N > 250) {                          // avoid high frequency noise
  if ( (Signal > thresh) && (Pulse == false) && (N > (IBI / 5) * 3) ) {
    Pulse = true;                       // set the Pulse flag when we
                                        think there is a pulse
    digitalWrite(blinkPin, LOW);        // turn on  LED
    IBI = sampleCounter - lastBeatTime; // measure time between beats
                                        in mS
    lastBeatTime = sampleCounter;       // keep track of time for next
                                        pulse

    if (secondBeat) {                   // if this is the second beat,
                                        if secondBeat == TRUE
      secondBeat = false;               // clear secondBeat flag
      for (int i = 0; i <= 9; i++) {    // seed the running total to
                                        get a realisitic BPM at startup

        rate[i] = IBI;
      }
    }
    if (firstBeat) {                    // if it's the first time we found
                                        a beat, if firstBeat == TRUE
      firstBeat = false;                // clear firstBeat flag
      secondBeat = true;                // set the second beat flag
      //sei();                          // enable interrupts again
      return;                           // IBI value is unreliable so
                                        discard it

    }
    // keep a running total of the last 10 IBI values
    word runningTotal = 0;              // clear the runningTotal variable

    for (int i = 0; i <= 8; i++) {      // shift data in the rate array
      rate[i] = rate[i + 1];            // and drop the oldest IBI value
      runningTotal += rate[i];          // add up the 9 oldest IBI values
    }
    rate[9] = IBI;                      // add the latest IBI to the
                                        rate array
    runningTotal += rate[9];            // add the latest IBI to
                                        runningTotal
    runningTotal /= 10;                 // average the last 10 IBI values
    BPM = 60000 / runningTotal;         // how many beats can fit into
                                        a minute? that's BPM!
    // reduce to 83% based on comparison
    BPM= (BPM * 83)/100;
    QS = true;                          // set Quantified Self flag
    // QS FLAG IS NOT CLEARED INSIDE THIS ISR
  }
}
```

```
  if (Signal < thresh && Pulse == true) {   // when the values are going
                                             down, the beat is over
     digitalWrite(blinkPin, HIGH);           // turn off pin 13 LED
     Pulse = false;                          // reset the Pulse flag so we can
                                             do it again

     amp = P - T;                            // get amplitude of the pulse wave
     thresh = amp / 2 + T;                   // set thresh at 50% of the amplitude
     P = thresh;                             // reset these for next time
     T = thresh;
  }

  if (N > 2500) {                            // if 2.5 seconds go by without
a beat
     thresh = 512;                           // set thresh default
     P = 512;                                // set P default
     T = 512;                                // set T default
     lastBeatTime = sampleCounter;           // bring the lastBeatTime up to date
     firstBeat = true;                       // set these to avoid noise
     secondBeat = false;                     // when we get the heartbeat back
  }

  //sei();                                   // enable interrupts when youre done!
}// end isr
```

Reviewing the Arduino IDE Serial Monitor Results

Listing 5-5 shows the output from the Serial Monitor on the Arduino IDE as you run the software. Note that this code was run after joining the IBM Bluemix IOT as shown later in this chapter. If you haven't joined the Bluemix IOT yet, then you will see an "authentication failed" error every time that the IOTPulse software tries to contact Bluemix.

Listing 5-5. Serial Monitor Output

```
IOTPulse IBM Bluemix IOT
----------------
Connecting to gracie........
Local WiFi connected, IP address: 192.168.1.117
*** Heart-Beat Happened *** BPM: 92 IBI: 534
*** Heart-Beat Happened *** BPM: 91 IBI: 630
*** Heart-Beat Happened *** BPM: 92 IBI: 468
*** Heart-Beat Happened *** BPM: 91 IBI: 590
*** Heart-Beat Happened *** BPM: 92 IBI: 516
*** Heart-Beat Happened *** BPM: 91 IBI: 548
*** Heart-Beat Happened *** BPM: 91 IBI: 530
*** Heart-Beat Happened *** BPM: 91 IBI: 556
*** Heart-Beat Happened *** BPM: 91 IBI: 540
*** Heart-Beat Happened *** BPM: 91 IBI: 530
```

```
*** Heart-Beat Happened *** BPM: 90 IBI: 586
*** Heart-Beat Happened *** BPM: 92 IBI: 538
*** Heart-Beat Happened *** BPM: 90 IBI: 540
*** Heart-Beat Happened *** BPM: 91 IBI: 564
IOT Delta time =10000002
Reconnecting client to 4183lj.messaging.internetofthings.ibmcloud.com
.
Sending IOTPulse payload: {"d":{"IOTPulse":"IP1","VER":4,"SC":1,"BPM":91,"I
BI":564,"BC":14}}
BlueMix IOT Publish ok
*** Heart-Beat Happened *** BPM: 87 IBI: 564
*** Heart-Beat Happened *** BPM: 87 IBI: 574
*** Heart-Beat Happened *** BPM: 87 IBI: 546
*** Heart-Beat Happened *** BPM: 87 IBI: 566
*** Heart-Beat Happened *** BPM: 87 IBI: 572
*** Heart-Beat Happened *** BPM: 87 IBI: 584
*** Heart-Beat Happened *** BPM: 87 IBI: 570
*** Heart-Beat Happened *** BPM: 87 IBI: 582
*** Heart-Beat Happened *** BPM: 87 IBI: 590
*** Heart-Beat Happened *** BPM: 86 IBI: 582
*** Heart-Beat Happened *** BPM: 86 IBI: 572
*** Heart-Beat Happened *** BPM: 85 IBI: 610
*** Heart-Beat Happened *** BPM: 85 IBI: 572
IOT Delta time =10000009
Reconnecting client to 4183lj.messaging.internetofthings.ibmcloud.com
.
Sending IOTPulse payload: {"d":{"IOTPulse":"IP1","VER":4,"SC":2,"BPM":85,"I
BI":572,"BC":27}}
BlueMix IOT Publish ok
*** Heart-Beat Happened *** BPM: 108 IBI: 456
*** Heart-Beat Happened *** BPM: 106 IBI: 562
*** Heart-Beat Happened *** BPM: 103 IBI: 568
*** Heart-Beat Happened *** BPM: 101 IBI: 574
*** Heart-Beat Happened *** BPM: 98 IBI: 576
*** Heart-Beat Happened *** BPM: 96 IBI: 582
```

Figure 5-8 shows the completed IOTPulse device in the case. Note the holes on the top to view the LEDs on the ESP8266 board. Figure 5-9 shows the pulse sensor clipped on an ear. Notice the green LED used for sensing the pulse rate in the ear.

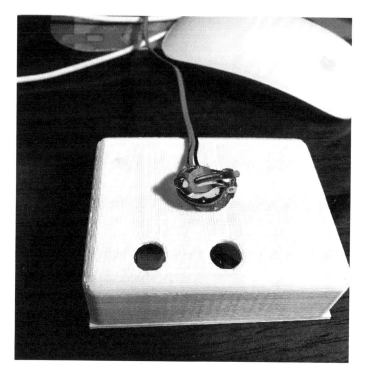

Figure 5-8. IOTPulse in Case

Figure 5-9. IOTPulse Sensor on Ear

172

Joining IBM Bluemix and the IoT Foundation

The IBM BlueMix and the IoT Foundation are the two key IOT cloud services we will be using to connect up the IOTPulse device to the cloud. The tasks that need to be done to connect up mostly have to do with setting up user accounts and putting billing information into the system. Note that we are using the free levels of the Bluemix system, but IBM still requires billing information. The most important technical information we will gather is how to authenticate our IOT device to the IBM cloud. Figure 5-10 describes the overall architecture of the Bluemix/IoT Foundation cloud application.

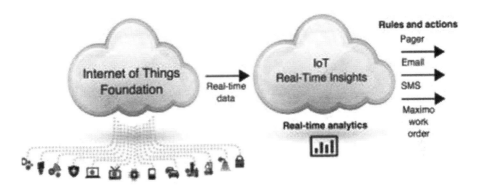

Figure 5-10. IBM Bluemix Block Diagram

The IoT Foundation is the IBM Bluemix service that we will need to hook up the ESP8266 to the Bluemix cloud service. You will need to create an IBM ID account. You can do so on the Bluemix home page shown in Figure 5-11.

173

Figure 5-11. IBM Bluemix First Page

The steps to join IBM Bluemix are the following:

1. Create an IBM ID account here;

2. Validate your account through the IBM sent e-mail;

3. Go to the IBM Bluemix site and click Log In;

4. Sign in on the login page;

5. Go to the Bluemix Dashboard;

6. Click USE SERVICES OR APIS;

7. Add the Internet of Things Foundation Service (It is WAY down at the bottom of the list on the web page).

You should then have a screen similar to the one in Figure 5-12, with the exception of the "IoT Real-Time Insights" panel, which will be added to your Bluemix account later in this chapter.

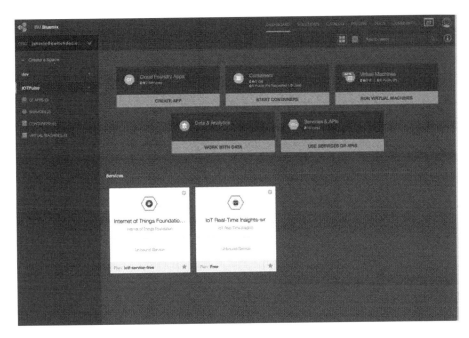

Figure 5-12. *Bluemix Dashboard*

Sending your Data to Bluemix

First of all, what do we send up to Bluemix from the ESP8266? It turns out the data protocols are pretty straightforward There are two major protocols that require descriptions.

MQTT and JSON.

MQTT

MQTT is a publish-subscribe-based "light weight" messaging protocol for use on top of the TCP/IP protocol, such as the WiFi packets that we are using in this project. It is designed for connections with remote locations where a "small code footprint" is required or the network bandwidth is limited. Both of these conditions are met with an ESP8266 IOT design, so it makes sense to use. There is also an excellent library available for MQTT for the Arduino IDE [https://github.com/knolleary/pubsubclient]. The publish-subscribe messaging pattern requires a message broker. The broker is responsible for distributing messages to interested clients based on the topic of a message (Figure 5-13).

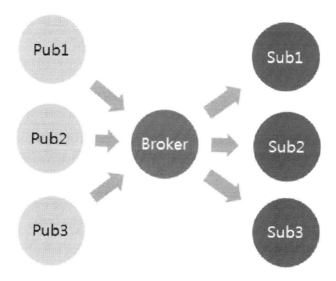

Figure 5-13. MQTT Publish-Subscribe Protocol

Publish-subscribe is a pattern where senders of messages, called publishers (in this case our ESP8266 is the publisher), don't program the messages to be sent directly to subscribers, but instead characterize message payloads into classes without the specific knowledge of which subscribers the messages are sent to. Similarly, subscribers (the IBM Bluemix IOT in this case) will only receive messages that are of interest without specific knowledge of which publishers there are. The IBM Bluemix operates as the broker in this system and routes the published data to the appropriate subscribers inside of Bluemix.

JSON Data Payload

JSON is an open standard format that uses human-readable text to transmit data objects consisting of attribute–value pairs. It is the primary data format used for asynchronous browser/server communication, largely replacing XML. XML is a "heavier" protocol that is also hierarchical in nature, but with a great deal more redundancy that JSON. Yes, there are class wars going on for people that advocate JSON over XML, but in today's world of higher speed communication, it rarely matters. You can make the argument that the higher data density of JSON is a better choice for IOT applications.

Here is an example of the data packet we are using in the ESP8266 Bluemix code in JSON for the LightSwarm data payload:

```
{"d":
    {
        "LightSwarm IOT":"LS1",
        "sampleCount":2118,
        "lightValue":383
    }
}
```

Authentication

We need to have a secure method of authenticating that our ESP8266 device is allowed to put data into the right slots inside the IBM Bluemix. This is done in our case by exchanging a cryptographic token that was generated by Bluemix and included in our ESP8266 code.

To do this we need to go back to the Bluemix account that you set up in the previous posting and complete the following steps:

1. Click the Internet of Things Foundation icon on the Bluemix dashboard.

2. Next, click the Launch dashboard button under "Connect your devices" (Figure 5-14).

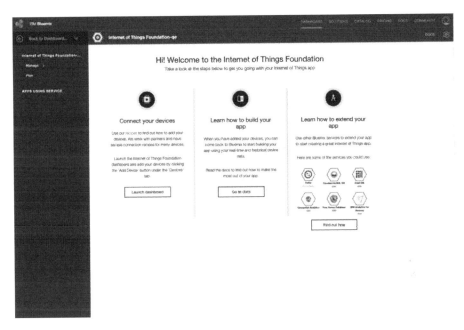

Figure 5-14. *Connect your Devices to Bluemix*

3. Go to the Devices Tab and "Add Device" down at the bottom of the page.

4. Click "Create Device Type," and the screen in Figure 5-15 appears.

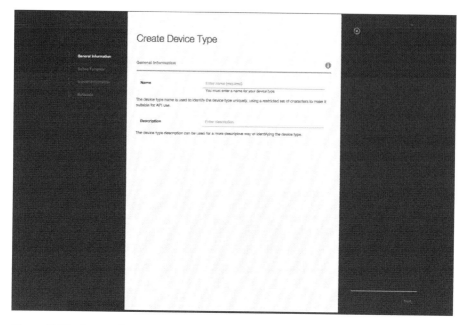

Figure 5-15. *Create Bluemix Device Type*

We would suggest you use IOTPulse-01 for the name of the device type.

Move through the rest of the steps. There are many configuration options that nearly all can be left blank in our current application. You are required to have a device type and a device ID.

When the device has been created, you'll see the Device Credentials page. Be sure to save those details, as they are used to authenticate your ESP8266 Arduino IDE sketch in in the next step (we have not found any way of recovering these credentials from the Bluemix system). Obviously, don't use the credentials in Figure 5-16. They will not work. You need to create your own.

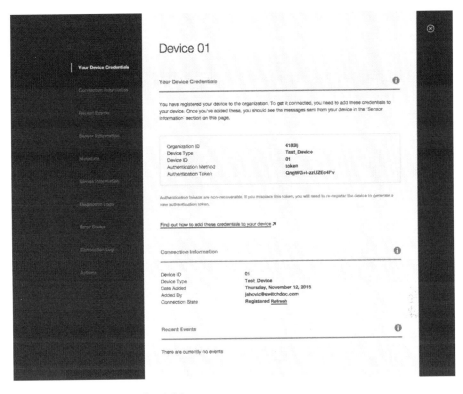

Figure 5-16. *Bluemix Credential Screen*

Displaying Real-Time Data on the IBM Bluemix IOT Platform

In order to get a display going in the Bluemix platform, we need to connect our device to the IoT Real-Time Insights service on Bluemix. The following sections discuss this.

Adding Real-Time Insights

Step 1: Add the IoT Real-Time Insights service to your Bluemix dashboard. Open the Bluemix dashboard (the first dashboard after login) and click "USE SERVICES OR APIS" and add the IoT Real-time Insights as a service. It is way down at the bottom of the page. You will then see the screen in Figure 5-17.

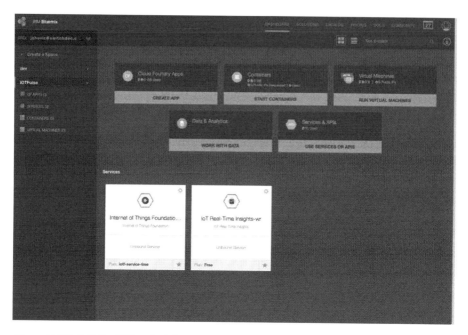

Figure 5-17. *IoT Real-Time Insights*

Step 2: Connect our device to the IoT Real-Time Insights Page by generating an API key and then generating a data source. Click the IoT Real-Time Insights block shown in Figure 5-16.

Step 3: Generate the API keys for using the Data Source and create API keys to connect the two services (IoT Foundation and IoT Real-Time Display):

1. From the Bluemix dashboard, click the Internet of Things tile.

2. Click **Launch dashboard** to open the Internet of Things Foundation dashboard.

3. Navigate to Access > API Keys.

4. Click Generate API Key.

5. Make a note of the API Key, Authentication Token, and the Organization ID that is displayed at the top of the IoT Foundation dashboard. You use this information in IoT Real-Time Insights to connect the services. **These keys will remain displayed in the data source.**

Adding the Data Source

Adding the data source (our IOTPulse device) consists of the following (Figure 5-18):

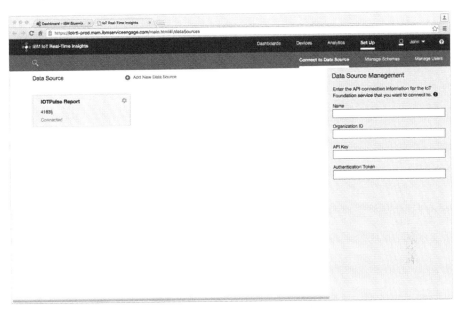

Figure 5-18. Adding the Data Source

1. Go to Devices > Manage Schemas and click Add new message schema.

2. Enter a name for the message schema: for example, IOTMessageSchema.

3. Click **Link new data source** and select the data source and device type that corresponds to your IoT Foundation instance and device. Event types for your device are here.

4. Add one or more data points that you want to include in the device dashboards (sampleCount and lightValue in our example).

5. The available data points are defined in the JSON payload of the messages that are sent by a device.

6. Click Select from connected device.

7. In the Add data points dialog, select one or more data points to add, and then click **OK**.

8. The selected data points are added with the description set to the name of the data point.

9. Then click the green arrow (on the left side of the screen) to save the information and create the data source.

181

Once all of the configuration data is in place and the authentication information is in place in the IOTPulse program, data should start to flow as shown in Figure 5-19.

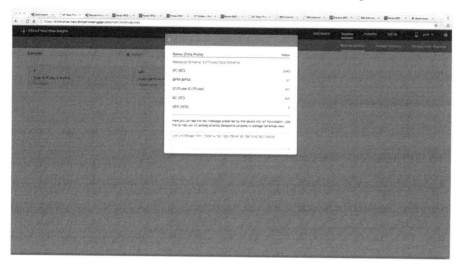

Figure 5-19. *IOT Data Starts to Flow*

Now we add the displays to visualize our data.

Adding the Dashboard to the IoT Real-Time Display

From the screen in Figure 5-20, click Launch IoT Real-Time Insights Dashboard in the lower right-hand column.

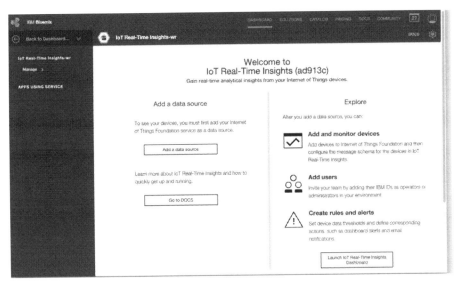

Figure 5-20. *IoT Real-Time Insights*

Click dashboard and browse dashboards. Add a new dashboard. Then do the following:

1. Add new component;

2. Select chart;

3. Add line to the chart;

4. Select your device and then select lightValue as the parameter;

5. Click the green arrow.

Figure 5-21 shows the IBM BlueMix screen for laying out your dashboard interface.

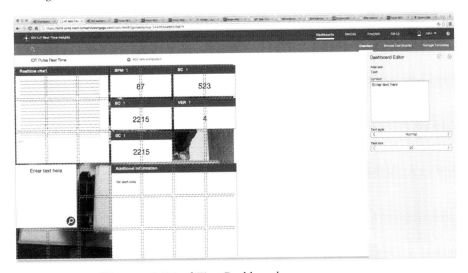

Figure 5-21. *Building your IoT Real-Time Dashboard*

If your ESP8266 is running and sending data up to the IBM Bluemix IOT, then you will see the values start to populate the graph, as shown in Figure 5-22.

Figure 5-22. *Bluemix IoT Real-Time Dashboard Operational*

Advanced Topics

The IBM cloud offerings have literally hundreds of options and possibilities for bringing your IOT data to the cloud. Below we show a few of these "apps" available on the Bluemix system. We will show how to graph your historical IOT data and introduce a complex, but very powerful, programming system, Node-RED.

Historical Data

Non-real-time historical data can also be viewed in Bluemix (Figure 5-23). This requires you to build an app (not as complex as you might think) and then deploy the app. A good tutorial for this is located on the IBM Bluemix web site [https://www.ng.bluemix.net/docs/starters/install_cli.html]. It does require you to install a command-line interface for Cloud Foundry on your computer.

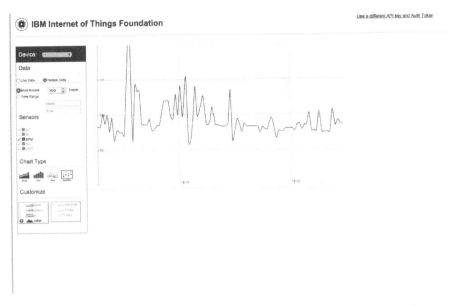

Figure 5-23. *Historical IOTPulse Data*

One thing this historical data graph of our pulse rate does show is that the data from IOTPulse could be improved by more filtering. The average of the heart rate looks good, but the jumps up and down look like noise, especially earlier in the graph.

Node-RED Applications

Node-RED is a graphical tool for wiring together devices, external APIs, and online services. You use a browser-based flow editor that makes it simple to wire together flows from an extensive library And it is easy to add your own nodes.

Node-RED is fully supported by IBM Bluemix. It is primarily an event-based software generation system. If an event happens (such as IOTPulse sending data), you can take that data and process it in various ways, send it to other applications, and store it in databases. Other inputs can cause displays to be updated, queries to be sent to databases, and many other events.

We built a small Node-RED application for IOTPulse shown in Figure 5-24.

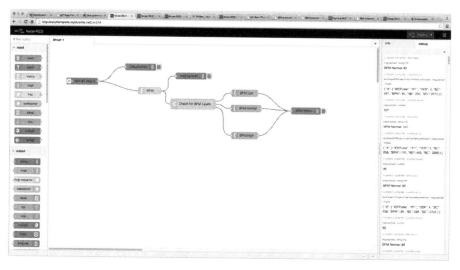

Figure 5-24. *Node-RED Application Flow for IOTPulse*

Watson Applications

One of the more exciting class of applications that can be built in Bluemix are those utilizing the IBM Watson software. All of the Watson services on the Bluemix platform are accessed via HTTP transfers known as REST services. REST stands for Representation State Transfer and is a common way of accessing web-based services.

Watson supports a number of very sophisticated services all available to your device and applications in Bluemix:

- Speech to Text

- Text to Speech

- Language Translation

- Support for User Dialogs

- Determining the "Tone" for Text

- Visual Recognition

- Image Analysis - Objects, People, and Text

Conclusion

The future of the IOT is data: how to gather it, how to transmit it, how to analyze and display it, and how to act on it. The IOTPulse project shows how to gather data and how to send it up to a cloud computing system for analysis and actions.

With a proper sensor, the IOTPulse project could be a commercial product. The sensor and analysis of the heart rate are definitely not medical grade, but still illustrates the principles of the IOT device and the device relationship with the IOT cloud.

CHAPTER 6

■ ■ ■

Using IOT for RFID and MQTT and the Raspberry Pi

Chapter Goal: Build an IOT device for Reading RFID Tags on Various Packages

Topics Covered in this Chapter:

- Introduction to RFID

- Introduction to MQTT Publish / Subscribe Systems and Servers

- Building a Raspberry Pi Based MQTT server

- Building an RFID Reader to Connect to the IOT

- Connecting your RFID Reader to your MQTT Raspberry Pi Server

- What to do with the RFID data on the Server

The world of IOT is dominated by small computers having small amounts of resources and power to communicate information with the rest of the world. MQTT is a publish-subscribe, lightweight protocol for IOT devices to communicate with the server and through the server, with each other. MQTT is also available for "mesh"-type networks, like Zigbee, that allow device-to-device communication. RFID (Radio Frequency IDentification) is an inexpensive way of reading uniquely numbered cards and tags via radio waves from short distances. RFID and its cousin, NFC (Near Field Communications) are showing up in more and more applications.

In this chapter, we build an RFID device and then connect through an MQTT publisher to an MQTT broker as in Chapter 5, but with the difference that we are replacing the IBM Bluemix MQTT broker with a Mosquitto broker running on a $20 Raspberry Pi.

IOT Characterization of This Project

As we discussed in Chapter 1, the first thing to do to understand an IOT project is to look at our six different aspects of IOT. ITORFID is a simpler project than our other four projects, but the dataflow is much more complex.

© John C. Shovic 2016
J. C. Shovic, *Raspberry Pi IoT Projects*, DOI 10.1007/978-1-4842-1377-3_6

Table 6-1 characterizes different aspects of the project. Ratings are from 1–10, 1 being the least suitable for IOT and 10 being the most suitable for IOT applications. This gives us a CPLPFC rating of 8.3. Great for learning and experimenting, and it could be deployed for some market applications.

Table 6-1. *IOT Characterization of the Project*

Aspect	Rating	Comments
Communications	9	WiFi connection to Internet -
Processor Power	9	80MHz XTensa Harvard Architecture CPU, ~80KB Data RAM / ~35KB of Instruction RAM / 200K ROM
Local Storage	8	4MB Flash (or 3MB file system!)
Power Consumption	8	~200mA transmitting, ~60mA receiving, noWiFi ~15mA, Standby ~1mA
Functionality	7	Partial Arduino Support (limited GPIO/Analog Inputs)
Cost	9	< $12 and getting cheaper

Note that the power consumption in this application could be dramatically reduced by adding a power down mode, say after 5 minutes of not using the RFID Reader.

What Is RFID Technology?

Radio Frequency Identification (RFID) is the use of radio waves to transfer data, specifically in the area of identifying and tracking tags attached to objects, people, and animals. Often the RFID Tag has no power supply and is activated and powered by radio waves beamed at the RFID Tag. This technology goes back to the 1940s and was first demonstrated by Theremin in the Soviet Union. Interestingly enough, he used this technology to put a covert listening device in the United States Embassy conference room in 1946. It was used for six years when in 1952, it was discovered that the seal contained a microphone and a resonant cavity that could be stimulated from an outside radio signal. While this used a resonant cavity that changed its shape when stimulated by sound waves, and hence modulated a reflected radio wave beamed at the unit, it is considered a predecessor to RFID technology.

[en.wikipedia.org/wiki/The_Thing_(listening_device)]

RFID tags can be active, passive (no battery power - we are using this technology in this chapter), and battery assisted passive. A passive tag contains no battery, instead using the radio energy transmitted by the RFID Reader. To operate a passive tag, it needs to be hit with a power level roughly one thousand times greater than the resulting signal transmissions.

When an RFID Tag is hit by a beam of radio waves from a transmitter, the passive tag is powered up and transmits back the tag identification number and other information. This may be a unique serial number, a stock or lot number, or other specific information. Since tags have unique numbers, the RFID system can read multiple tags simultaneously, with some clever programming of the receiver and transmitter.

There are a number of different RFID standards in common use. There are three standards for putting ID chips in pets, which of course are not compatible with each other and require different readers. The short-range tags we are using in this chapter operated at the low frequency of 125kHz and can go up to 100mm (Figure 6-1). Other tags can be picked up (with active RFID technology) up to 100 meters.

While RFID and NFC technologies are designed for short distance use, the addition of a large power transmitter and a large antenna can change the meaning of "short distance."

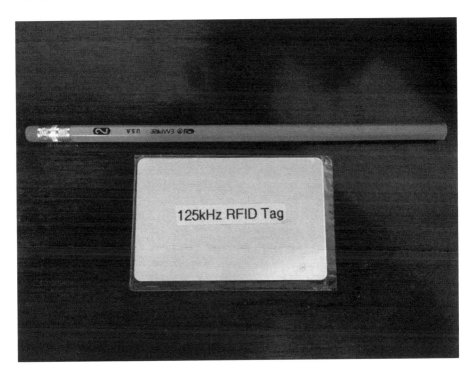

Figure 6-1. *125kHz Card-Shaped RFID Tag*

What Is MQTT?

In Chapter 5, we used an MQTT publisher module to talk to the IBM MQTT broker at IBM Bluemix.

To refresh the reader's memory, MQTT is a publish-subscribe-based "light weight" messaging protocol for use on top of the TCP/IP protocol, such as the WiFi packets that we are using in this project. It is designed for connections with remote locations where a "small code footprint" is required or the network bandwidth is limited.

Publish-subscribe is a pattern where senders of messages, called publishers (in this case our project IOTRFID is the publisher), don't program the messages to be sent directly to subscribers, but instead characterize message payloads into classes.

You can think of it as writing stories for a newspaper where you don't know who will be subscribing to the article.

Hardware Used for IOTRFID

There are there major parts to the hardware from the IOTRFID (Figure 6-2). The first is the ESP8266 Adafruit Huzzah that we have seen in previous chapters.

The RFID reading circuit is a small inexpensive board from Seeedstudio in China. The key reason this board was chosen was the fact it works on 3.3V (which is the same as the ESP8266) and requires no external components (well, yes, it does require an antenna that is included).

We also purchased a 125KHz RFID Tag from SparkFun. Be careful of the RFID Tag you buy. Not all are compatible.

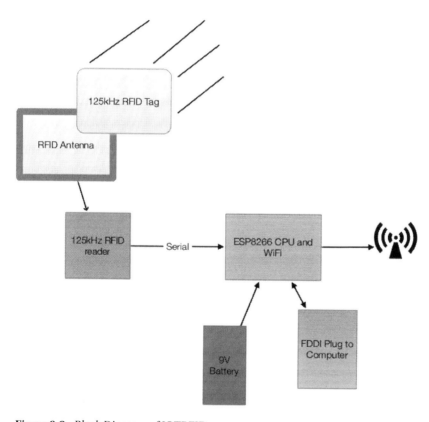

Figure 6-2. *Block Diagram of IOTRFID*

Building an MQTT Server on a Raspberry Pi

As described in Chapter 5, MQTT requires a message broker. The design pattern is this:

1. IOTRFID publishes a payload;

2. Raspberry Pi MQTT broker receives the payload;

3. Raspberry Pi MQTT broker disseminates to all subscribing objects (which may be different processes in the same machine - as in our case - or even different machines entirely.

In Chapter 5, we used the IBM Bluemix as the message broker. In the IOTRFID project we are going to build a message broker on the Raspberry Pi.

Figure 6-3 shows the dataflow in the entire application - including the Raspberry Pi. The dataflow in this application is basically one way: from the RFID Tag to the Raspberry Pi mosquitto server. Note, however, there are two channels available over the WiFi and you could send commands back to the IOTRFID project telling the user information about the part being inventoried. For example, you could display the destination for the box or the expiration date.

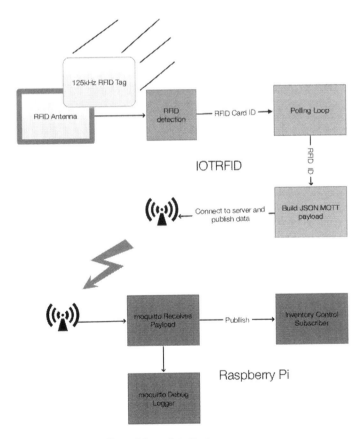

Figure 6-3. *Dataflow of Complete System*

There are a number of MQTT brokers available for different machines. For this project, we have selected one of the most popular and stable brokers, "Mosquitto." Note the two "t'"s in Mosquitto. The bane of spell checkers everywhere.

Mosquitto supports MQTT v3.1/3.1.1 and is easily installed on the Raspberry Pi and somewhat less easy to configure. Next we step through installing and configuring the Mosquitto broker.

The Software on the Raspberry Pi

We start by setting up the software on the Raspberry Pi. We do this so our IOTRFID has something to talk to when we set turn the IOTRFID on.

Installing the MQTT "Mosquitto"

Unfortunately, the Raspberry Pi normal "apt-get" archives do not contain the latest version of the Mosquitto software. If you don't install the latest version of the broker, you will get odd errors (because of version compatibility errors) and it will not work. So, the first thing is to open a Terminal window (or log in using ssh) to your Raspberry Pi and do the following:

```
sudo wget http://repo.mosquitto.org/debian/mosquitto-repo.gpg.key
sudo apt-key add mosquitto-repo.gpg.key
cd /etc/apt/sources.list.d/
sudo wget http://repo.mosquitto.org/debian/mosquitto-wheezy.list
sudo apt-get update
sudo apt-get install mosquitto
```

Next we can install the three parts of Mosquitto proper.

- mosquitto - the MQTT broker (or in other words, a server)

- mosquitto-clients – command-line clients, very useful in debugging

- python-mosquitto - the Python language bindings

Execute the following command to install these three parts:

```
sudo apt-get install mosquitto mosquitto-clients python-mosquitto
```

As is the case with most packages from Debian, the broker is immediately started. Since we have to configure it first, stop it:

```
sudo /etc/init.d/mosquitto stop
```

Configuring and Starting the Mosquitto Server

Before using Mosquitto, we need to set up the configuration file. The configuration file is located at /etc/mosquitto.

Open the file as follows:

```
sudo nano /etc/mosquitto/mosquitto.conf
```

You should see the following:

```
# Place your local configuration in /etc/mosquitto/conf.d/
#
# A full description of the configuration file is at
# /usr/share/doc/mosquitto/examples/mosquitto.conf.example

pid_file /var/run/mosquitto.pid

persistence true
persistence_location /var/lib/mosquitto/

log_dest file /var/log/mosquitto/mosquitto.log

include_dir /etc/mosquitto/conf.d
```

Change the "log_dest" line to:

```
log_dest topic
```

This puts the logging information as a "topic" so we can subscribe to it later on to see what is going on in our IOTRFID system.

Next add the following six lines:

```
log_type error
log_type warning
log_type notice
log_type information

connection_messages true
log_timestamp true
```

Now your /etc/mosquitto.conf files should look like this:

```
# Place your local configuration in /etc/mosquitto/conf.d/
#
# A full description of the configuration file is at
# /usr/share/doc/mosquitto/examples/mosquitto.conf.example

pid_file /var/run/mosquitto.pid

persistence true
persistence_location /var/lib/mosquitto/
```

```
log_dest topic

log_type error
log_type warning
log_type notice
log_type information

connection_messages true
log_timestamp true

include_dir /etc/mosquitto/conf.d
```

Starting the Mosquitto Server

Now start the mosquitto server:

```
sudo /etc/init.d/mosquitto start
```

The server should start, and you are ready to move on to testing.

Testing the Mosquitto Server

Open up two more terminal windows.

In Terminal window 1 type:

```
mosquitto_sub -d -t hello/world
```

In Terminal window 2 type:

```
mosquitto_pub -d -t hello/world -m "Hello from Terminal window 2!"
```

When you have done the second statement you should see this in the Terminal 1 window.

```
~ $ sudo mosquitto_sub -d -t hello/world
Client mosqsub/3014-LightSwarm sending CONNECT
Client mosqsub/3014-LightSwarm received CONNACK
Client mosqsub/3014-LightSwarm sending SUBSCRIBE (Mid: 1, Topic: hello/
world, QoS: 0)
Client mosqsub/3014-LightSwarm received SUBACK
Subscribed (mid: 1): 0
Client mosqsub/3014-LightSwarm received PUBLISH (d0, q0, r0, m0, 'hello/
world', ... (32 bytes))
Greetings from Terminal window 2
```

Now you are running the Mosquitto broker successfully.
Next, let's build the IOTRFID device.

Building the IOTRFID

The IOTRFID project consists of four major parts:

- ESP8266

- RFID Reader

- Software for the ESP8266

- Software for the Raspberry Pi

The purpose of this project is to prototype an inventory control system that uses RFID tags. The ESP8266 controls the RFID Reader and reports the RFID Tag to the Raspberry Pi server. We then use MQTT through the WiFi interface on the ESP8266 to send the inventory information to the Raspberry Pi. The Raspberry Pi could then use the RFID information to work with a database, alert the end customer, etc.

The Parts Needed

The IOTRFID can be assembled for about $35 from the sources in Table 6-2.

Table 6-2. Parts List for IOTRFID

Part Number	Count	Description	Approximate Cost per Board	Source
ESP8266 Huzzah Board	1	CPU / WiFi board	$10	www.adafruit.com/ products/2471
Mini 125kHz RFID Reader	1	125kHz RFID Serial Reader	$11	www.seeedstudio. com/depot/Mini- 125Khz-RFID-Module- External-LEDBuzzer- Port-70mm-Reading- Distance-p-1724.html
125kHz RFID Tags	1	RFID Tag compatible with Mini 125kHz RFID Reader	$2	www.sparkfun.com/ products/8310
FTDI Cable	1	Cable for programming the ESP8266 from PC/Mac	$11	www.switchdoc.com/ inexpensive-ftdi- cable-for-arduino- esp8266-includes- usb-cable/

Installing Arduino Support on the PC or Mac

Once again, the key to making this project work is the development software. While there are many ways of programming the ESP8266 (MicroPython [https://micropython.org], NodeMCU Lua interpreter [http://nodemcu.com] and the Arduino IDE (Integrated Development Environment) [https://www.arduino.cc/en/Main/Software]), we chose the Arduino IDE for its flexibility and the large number of sensors and device libraries available.

To install the Arduino IDE you need to do the following:

1. Download the Arduino IDE package for your computer and install the software [https://www.arduino.cc/en/Guide/HomePage].

2. Download the ESP libraries so you can use the Arduino IDE with the ESP breakout board. Adafruit has an excellent tutorial for installing the ESP8266 support for the Arduino IDE [https://learn.adafruit.com/adafruit-huzzah-esp8266-breakout/using-arduino-ide].

The Hardware

The main pieces of hardware in the swarm device are these:

- ESP8266 - CPU/WiFi Interface
- Mini 125kHz RFID Reader
- 9V Battery - Power
- FTDI Cable - Programming and Power

The ESP8266 communicates with the Raspberry Pi by using the WiFi interface. The ESP8266 uses a serial interface to communicate with the light sensor. The WiFi is a standard that is very common. The serial interface used is one wire (Tx line on the RFID Reader to Rx on the ESP8266 - Pin GPIO #4 on the ESP8266). In a serial interface, one bit at a time is sent along with stop and start bits for each byte. The data is sent at 9600 baud, which is an old way of saying about 9600 bits per second.

What Is This Sensor We Are Using?

The Mini 125kHz RFID Reader is a simple, inexpensive 125kHz RFID Tag reader with a range of about 70mm. Note that the range for a reader like this is set by a combination of the output power of the reader and the antenna design.

If you have a bigger antenna and more power, you can read RFID tags at a much larger distance. A quick check on the Web showed the record for passive 125kHz RFID tags is around 10 or 15 meters. Better antennas that are focused on a beam could do even better than this. Don't assume that someone cannot read the cards in your wallet if they really wanted to do that.

3D Printed Case

The 3D printed case for this project has a holder for a 9 volt battery, pylons to hold the antenna in place, a slot to mount the RFID Reader board, and pylons for the ESP8266. The code is for OpenSCAD, a free 3D CAD system that appeals to programmers. Figure 6-4 shows the 3D printed case with pylons for mounting the boards.

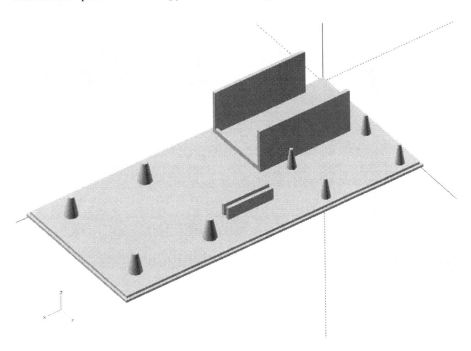

Figure 6-4. *3D Printed Case for the IOTRFID Project*

The following OpenSCAD code builds the mounting base step by step by merging basic shapes such as cubes and cones. We also build a stand to keep the battery from sliding across the base.

```
//
// IOT IOTFRFID Mounting Base
//
// SwitchDoc Labs
// February 2016
//

union()
{
```

```
cube([130,60,2]);
translate([-1,-1,0])
cube([132,62,1]);

// Mount for Battery

translate([-30,0,0])
union ()
{
translate([40,2,0])
cube([40,1.35,20]);
translate([40,26.10+3.3,0])
cube([40,1.5,20]);

// lips for battery
translate([79,2,0])
cube([1,28,4]);

// plyons for ESP8266

translate([70-1.0,35,0])
cylinder(h=10,r1=2.2, r2=1.35/2, $fn=100);
translate([70-1.0,56,0])
cylinder(h=10,r1=2.2, r2=1.35/2, $fn=100);
translate([70-34,35,0])
cylinder(h=10,r1=2.2, r2=1.35/2, $fn=100);
translate([70-34,56,0])
cylinder(h=10,r1=2.2, r2=1.35/2, $fn=100);
}

// stand for board

translate([15,40,0])
union ()
{
translate([40,2,0])
cube([20,1.35,7]);
translate([40,3.55+1.35,0])
cube([20,1.35,7]);
}
// plyons for RFID  board

translate([50,0,0])
union()
{
translate([33+36.0,10,0])
cylinder(h=10,r1=3.2, r2=2.40/2, $fn=100);
translate([33+36.0,50,0])
cylinder(h=10,r1=3.2, r2=2.40/2, $fn=100);
```

```
translate([36,10,0])
cylinder(h=10,r1=3.2, r2=2.40/2, $fn=100);
translate([36,50,0])
cylinder(h=10,r1=3.2, r2=2.40/2, $fn=100);
}

}
```

The Full Wiring List

Figure 6-5 shows the back of the Mini 125kHz RFID Reader to clearly display the pin labels on the back of the board.

Figure 6-5. *Closeup of Mini RFID Board*

Following is the complete wiring list for the IOTRFID project. As you wire it, check off each wire for accuracy.

The Key for Table 6-3 is below. Table 6-3 contains all the wiring information for building the IOTRFID. Follow it closely to make your project work the first time. This table contains all of the individual wiring connections to complete the project.

ESP8266 Huzzah Board: **ESP8266**

Mini 125kHz RFID Reader: **RFIDBoard**

9V Battery: **9VBat**

Table 6-3. *Wiring List for the IOTRFID Project*

ESP8266 Huzzah Board (ESP8266)		
From	**To**	**Description**
ESP8266 / GND	RFIDBoard /G	Ground for RFID Reader board
ESP8266 / 3V	RFIDBoard /V	3.3V Power for RFID Board
ESP8266 / #5	RFIDBoard /Rx	RFID Board Receiver (not used in this project)
ESP8266 / #4	RFIDBoard /Tx	RFID Board Serial Transmitter
ESP8266 / GND	9VBat / "-" terminal (minus terminal)	Ground for battery
ESP8266 / VBat	9VBat / "+" terminal (plus 9V)	9V from battery
RFIDBoard / T1	RFID Antenna JST2 Plug	Lead from Antenna - Push plug over T1 and T2 - order doesn't matter
RFIDBoard / T2	RFID Antenna JST2 Plug	Lead from Antenna - Push plug over T1 and T2 - order doesn't matter

Figure 6-6 shows the JST2 Plug pushed over the two pins on the RFID board connecting the RFID board with the Antenna.

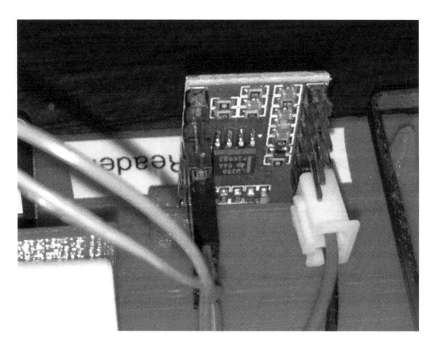

Figure 6-6. *Closeup of RFID Antenna JST2 Plug*

Your completed IOTRFID project should look similar to Figure 6-7.

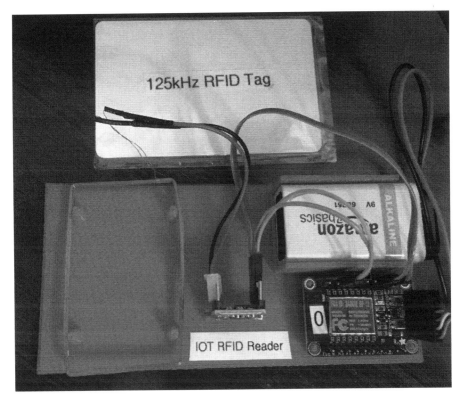

Figure 6-7. *The Completed IOTRFID Project*

The Software for the IOTRFID Project

No computer-based project is complete without the software to make the computer and board perform the functions designed. The main code IOTRFID is very short and makes good use of existing libraries.

The Libraries

In this project, we are using two libraries. Because we didn't have to modify the libraries to make them work with the ESP8266, we have not reproduced them here. The two libraries are the following:

> seeedRFID - The library for interfacing the ESP8266 to the RFID Reader. Basically a simple shell around the SoftSerial Arduino libraries. [https://github.com/Seeed-Studio/RFID_Library]

> PubSubClient - A simple client for MQTT. This is a very
> usable and well-documented library. We use this library to
> talk to the MQTT server (mosquitto) on the Raspberry Pi.
> [http://pubsubclient.knolleary.net]

The Main Software

The ESP8266 Arduino IDE software for this project is relatively straightforward. You will see
some similarities to the IBM Bluemix software in the last chapter. The main difference is that
you are now doing both ends of the MQTT connections. Remember to put your own WiFi
access point and password in the code as well as entering the IP address of your Raspberry Pi.

The general flow of the software consists of first initializing the WiFi connection and
the RFID hardware and then going into a loop, checking for RFID Tag events.

```
/*
    SwitchDoc Labs Code for IOT RFID
    IOT RFID uses publish subscribe to communicate to Raspberry Pi
    January 2016
*/

// BOF preprocessor bug prevent - insert on top of your arduino-code
#if 1
__asm volatile ("nop");
#endif

// Board options

#pragma GCC diagnostic ignored "-Wwrite-strings"

extern "C" {
#include "user_interface.h"
}
#include <ESP8266WiFi.h>
#include "PubSubClient.h"

#include "seeedRFID.h"

#define RFID_RX_PIN 4
#define RFID_TX_PIN 5

#undef TEST

SeeedRFID RFID(RFID_RX_PIN, RFID_TX_PIN);
RFIDdata tag;

int count = 0;    // counter for buffer array

//  Variables
```

```
int blinkPin = 0;                        // pin to blink led at each reception of
                                         RFID code


#include "Utils.h"

//-----------------------------------------------------------------------
//Local WiFi Variables

const char* ssid = "YOURWIFIACCESSPOINT";
const char* password = "YOURWIFIPASSWORD";

#define IOTRFIDVERSION 005
// Raspberry Pi Information

#define ORG "switchdoc"
#define DEVICE_TYPE "IOTRFID-01"
#define DEVICE_ID "1"
#define TOKEN "ul!fjH!y8yOgDREmsA"

// setup for IOT Raspberry Pi

char server[] = "192.168.1.40";   // Replace with YOUR RASPBERRY IP Number
char topic[] = "IOTRFID";
char authMethod[] = "use-token-auth";
char token[] = TOKEN;
char clientId[] = "IOTRFID";

void callback(char* topic, byte* payload, unsigned int length) {
  Serial.println("callback invoked from IOT RFID");
}

WiFiClient wifiClient;
PubSubClient client(server, 1883, callback, wifiClient);

void setup() {
  // put your setup code here, to run once:

  pinMode(0, OUTPUT);

  Serial.begin(9600);                    // we agree to talk fast!

  Serial.println("----------------");
  Serial.println("IOTRFID publish/subscribe Inventory");
  Serial.println("----------------");

  // signal start of code - three quick blinks
  blinkLED(3, 250);
```

```
  Serial.print("Connecting to WiFi ");

  if (strcmp (WiFi.SSID().c_str(), ssid) != 0) {
    WiFi.begin(ssid, password);
  }
  while (WiFi.status() != WL_CONNECTED) {
    delay(500);
    Serial.print(".");
  }
  Serial.println("");

  Serial.print("Local WiFi connected, IP address: ");
  Serial.println(WiFi.localIP());

  blinkLED(5, 500);
}

void loop() {
  // put your main code here, to run repeatedly:

  count = 0;

  if (!!!client.connected()) {
    Serial.print("Reconnecting client to ");
    Serial.println(server);
while (!!!client.connect(clientId)) {
      Serial.print(".");
      delay(500);
    }
    Serial.println();
  }

  // Check for RFID available

  String payload;

  if (RFID.isAvailable())
  {
    tag = RFID.data();
    Serial.print("RFID card number read: ");
    Serial.println(RFID.cardNumber());
#ifdef TEST
    Serial.print("RFID raw data: ");
    for (int i = 0; i < tag.dataLen; i++) {
      Serial.print(tag.raw[i], HEX);
      Serial.print('\t');
    }
#endif

    // Sending payload
```

```
payload = "{\"d\":{\"IOTRFID\":\"IR1\",";
payload += "\"VER\":\"";
payload += IOTRFIDVERSION;
payload += "\",\"RFID_ID\":\"";
payload += String(RFID.cardNumber());
payload += "\"";
payload += "}}";

// check for message

Serial.println(payload.length());

count = 0;

if (payload.length() >= 53) // good message
{
  Serial.print("Sending IOTRFID payload: ");
  Serial.println(payload);

  if (client.publish(topic, (char*) payload.c_str())) {
    Serial.println("IOTRFID Publish ok");
    blinkLED(1, 500);
  } else {
    Serial.println("IOTRFID Publish failed");
    blinkLED(2, 500);
  }
}

else
{
  delay(500);
}
}

  yield();    // This is necessary for the ESP8266 to do the background tasks
}
```

Testing the IOTRFID System

Using the Arduino IDE, flash the ESP8266 with the IOTRFID software above.

After it has been flashed, you should see the following on the Arduino serial monitor:

```
----------------
IOTRFID publish/subscribe Inventory
----------------
Connecting to WiFi ......
Local WiFi connected, IP address: 192.168.1.135
Reconnecting client to 192.168.1.40
```

Leave the IOTRFID running for now.

Setting Up the Mosquitto Debug Window

Go back into Terminal window 1 from earlier in the chapter and hold down the control key and click "c" (control-c) to kill the running process from the previous step. If you had closed it, open up another Terminal window and following the instructions below.

Build a python file for our debug and logging subscription to the Mosquitto broker:

nano IOTRFIDLogSubscribe.py

Enter the following code:

```
#
# SwitchDoc Labs
#
# Display logging subscription
#
# January 2016
#

import paho.mqtt.client as mqtt

# The callback for when the client receives a CONNACK response from the
server.
def on_connect(client, userdata, flags, rc):
    print("Connected with result code "+str(rc))

    # Subscribing in on_connect() means that if we lose the connection and
    # reconnect then subscriptions will be renewed.
    client.subscribe("$SYS/broker/log/#");

# The callback for when a PUBLISH message is received from the server.
def on_message(client, userdata, msg):
    print(msg.topic+" "+str(msg.payload))

client = mqtt.Client()
client.on_connect = on_connect
client.on_message = on_message

client.connect("localhost", 1883, 60)

# Blocking call that processes network traffic, dispatches callbacks and
# handles reconnecting.
# Other loop*() functions are available that give a threaded interface and a
# manual interface.
client.loop_forever()
```

Then run the code by typing this:

```
sudo python IOTRFIDLogSubscribe.py
```

We use "sudo" to make sure that python is running with root privileges to avoid any potential permissions issues.

If you left your IOTRFID running, you will see this:

```
Connected with result code 0
SYS/broker/log/N 1454535157: Client IOTRFID has exceeded timeout,
disconnecting.
$SYS/broker/log/N 1454535157: Socket error on client IOTRFID, disconnecting.
$SYS/broker/log/N 1454535157: New connection from 192.168.1.135 on port
1883.
$SYS/broker/log/N 1454535157: New client connected from 192.168.1.135 as
IOTRFID (c1, k15).
```

This means that your IOTRFID is connected to the Mosquitto MQTT broker.

Next, let's go to another Terminal window and set up a subscriber on the Raspberry Pi to our IOTRFID device.

Set Up a Subscriber on the Raspberry Pi

In another Terminal window on the Raspberry Pi, build another python file by typing the following:

```
sudo nano IOTRFIDSubscriber.py
```

Enter the following code:

```
#
#
# IOTRFID Subscribe Module
#
# Receives inventory message from IOTRFID
# SwitchDoc Labs January 2016
#

import json

import paho.mqtt.client as mqtt

def filter_non_printable(str):
  return ''.join([c for c in str if ord(c) > 31 or ord(c) == 9])

# The callback for when the client receives a CONNACK response from the
server.
def on_connect(client, userdata, flags, rc):
    print("Connected with result code "+str(rc))
```

```
    # Subscribing in on_connect() means that if we lose the connection and
    # reconnect then subscriptions will be renewed.
    client.subscribe("IOTRFID/#")

# The callback for when a PUBLISH message is received from the server.
def on_message(client, userdata, msg):
    print(msg.topic+" "+str(msg.payload))
    result = json.loads(filter_non_printable(msg.payload))  # result is now a
dict / filter start and stop characters
    InventoryRFID = result['d']['RFID_ID']

    print
    print("IOTRFID Inventory Number Received From ID#"+result['d']
['IOTRFID'])
    print("Inventory Item = " + InventoryRFID)
    print

client = mqtt.Client()
client.on_connect = on_connect
client.on_message = on_message

client.connect("localhost", 1883, 60)

# Blocking call that processes network traffic, dispatches callbacks and
# handles reconnecting.
# Other loop*() functions are available that give a threaded interface and a
# manual interface.
client.loop_forever()
```

Execute the code by typing this:

```
sudo python IOTRFIDSubscriber.py
```

You will see the following:

```
Connected with result code 0
```

Next, we will run the full system test.

Testing the Entire IOTRFID System

Take your RFID Tag card and wave it over the IOTRFID antenna as shown in Figure 6-8.

Figure 6-8. *RFID Tag Card over the IOTRFID Device*

If your IOTRFID is running, you should see something similar to the following in the Arduino IDE Serial Window:

```
Reconnecting client to 192.168.1.40

RFID card number read: 2413943
53
Sending IOTRFID payload: {"d":{"IOTRFID":"IR1","VER":"5","RFID_
ID":"2413943"}}
IOTRFID Publish ok
```

And over in terminal 2, you should see something similar to this:

```
IOTRFID {"d":{"IOTRFID":"IR1","VER":"5","RFID_ID":"2413943"}}
IOTRFID Inventory Number Recieved From ID#IR1
Inventory Item = 2413943
```

If you look at the debug window in Terminal 1, you should see something like this if you have no errors:

```
$SYS/broker/log/N 1454536590: New client connected from 192.168.1.135 as
IOTRFID (c1, k15).
```

```
$SYS/broker/log/N 1454536615: Client IOTRFID has exceeded timeout,
disconnecting.
$SYS/broker/log/N 1454536615: Socket error on client IOTRFID, disconnecting.
$SYS/broker/log/N 1454536615: New connection from 192.168.1.135 on port
1883.
$SYS/broker/log/N 1454536615: New client connected from 192.168.1.135 as
IOTRFID (c1, k15).
```

You just successfully published an MQTT message form IOTRFID to the Mosquitto MQTT broker on the Raspberry Pi and received it on a MQTT subscriber in Terminal 2.

You have connected your IOT device into your own MQTT broker just as you did with IBM Bluemix in the previous chapter.

What to Do with the RFID Data on the Server

In our subscriber example, we have a very small piece of code that is handling the RFID inventory information coming in from IOTRFID. This section is the "on_message" function shown below:

```
# The callback for when a PUBLISH message is received from the server.
def on_message(client, userdata, msg):
    print(msg.topic+" "+str(msg.payload))
    result = json.loads(filter_non_printable(msg.payload))  # result is now a
dict / filter start and stop characters
    InventoryRFID = result['d']['RFID_ID']

    print
    print("IOTRFID Inventory Number Received From ID#"+result['d']
['IOTRFID'])
    print("Inventory Item = " + InventoryRFID)
    print
```

While we are just printing it out to the screen, if you were building an actual inventory system, this function is where you would call the database, action programs, and other publish-subscribe nodes that need to be notified that this piece of inventory has been scanned.

Conclusion

It should be somewhat surprising that we can duplicate a significant amount of the functionality of IBM Bluemix with less than only $50 worth of hardware. In truth, we have done that with this project. However, there are lots of things missing in our implementation versus the IBM Bluemix system. Our system has no redundancy, no way to scale it up to tens of thousands of devices, is lacking a real administrative control panel, and has not addressed the very important issue of computer security and hackability.

The concepts we have explored in this chapter should give the reader some very solid insights into the technology and turn a black box (like IBM Bluemix) into something that is easier to understand.

As far as computer security goes for IOT devices, this is an excellent segue into our next chapter, "Computer Security and the IOT."

CHAPTER 7

Computer Security and the IOT

Chapter Goal: Understand the Basics of IOT Computer Security

Topics Covered in This Chapter:

- The Top Five Things to Worry About

- What Computer Security Is

- Computer Security for Communications

- Computer Security for Hardware Devices

- Protecting your Users

Why are we worried about computer security on the IOT?

Hackers are everywhere. They attack our banks. They attack our stores (think Target). They are trying to attack our infrastructure (power, water, sewer, etc.). Now, with the advent of IOT, they have a gateway into your home.

Guess what? They are going to attack your IOT device. You may think you are safe because you are not very important (see no. 2 below - not being important is not a good defense); they will attack.

Understand one very important fact. Hackers rarely attack something specific. They use programs to attack thousands and tens of thousands of things at a time. Then they just wait for the results. If you are exposed on the Internet, they WILL find you. Your job is to make sure they can't do anything important about it.

Who are the hackers? There are the black hat people trying to make money from attacks or ransomware. There are nation-states doing this (and not just the United States, China, and Russia, either. North Korea and many other nations have programs). It's just not that expensive to do and the Internet gives you access to anywhere.

There are white hat hackers that are trying to find and fix security issues in programs and on the Internet. These people are trying to actually help the problem.

Oh, and then there is a whole other category of people that are somewhere in the middle. Gray hats if you like. These are people that are not really sure what they are doing. People can download hacking programs and run them without having any idea what is going on. These people are called "Script Kiddies" and can cause all sorts of damage on purpose or not.

© John C. Shovic 2016

J. C. Shovic, *Raspberry Pi IoT Projects*, DOI 10.1007/978-1-4842-1377-3_7

IOT: Top Five Things to Know About IOT Computer Security

The author has run a computer security company and has taught computer security and information warfare at the undergraduate and graduate level at several universities. In this chapter I am taking a different look at computer security than most technical books. While I am discussing methods of encryption and authentication, I am also taking a top-level view of the problem and a realistic view of what can and can't be done with the small computers that make up the IOT.

With that, let's start with my thoughts about the Top Five Things to Know About IOT Computer Security.

Number 1: This is *important.* You can prove your application *is insecure,* but you can't prove your application *is secure.*

"What? That doesn't make any sense. My application only has 200 lines of code in it and I can see that it is secure!"

There are two things to consider here. First of all is that those 200 lines have been compiled by a compiler that has 100,000+ lines of code. The operating system you are running on has at least 25,000 lines of code (yes, even an Arduino) and millions of lines of code in a Raspberry Pi or Windows machine. Your 200 lines of code interact with tens of thousands of lines of code. You don't know how big your own program is. You don't know about the compiler. You don't know about the operating system. Yes, some micro-controllers allow you to set up everything, but in today's development systems this is the exception, not the rule.

The second thing to consider is a proven theorem from Matt Bishop's excellent book [Computer Security: Art and Science, Matt Bishop] on Computer Security: "It is undecidable whether a given state of a given protection system is safe for a given generic right."

What does this mean? It means that "You can tell if your computer program is insecure, but you can't know if it is secure."

Ouch.

Number 2: Security through Obscurity Is Not Security

An IOT system that relies on secrecy of the implementations or components of the system is not security. Obscurity can be part of a defense in-depth strategy but should not be relied on to provide security. Yes, someone can take your design and reverse engineer it and find out everything about it. Using a different port for SSH doesn't even slow down hackers these days. People can snoop on what you are sending and figure it out. Your system needs to rely on the key to your system and not the structure of the lock.

Number 3: Always Connected? Always Vulnerable.

Every moment that your IOT device is connected to the Internet or the network is a moment that it can be attacked. Keep your device off the network as much as possible. This saves power, too, which is often a defining design criteria.

Number 4: Focus On What Is *Important* to Be Secure in your IOT Application

Does a hacker care that the temperature in your aquarium is 85 degrees? Probably not. Do you want them to be able to change the temperature in your aquarium? Probably not. Do you want your front door lock (that is connected to the Internet?) to be secure? Yes, all the time. And no, you don't want hackers to be able to tell if the door is locked or unlocked. Just remember all the encryption in the world doesn't matter if a person has the key. In this case, either a physical key or a cryptographic key. Both can open your door. In our door lock IOT application, we must keep the key safe.

Number 5: Computer Security Rests on Three Main Aspects: Confidentiality, Integrity, and Availability

Confidentiality is defined as the concealment of information or resources. Keeping things secret (like keys) so the hackers can't use them.

Integrity is defined as the trustworthiness of the data or resources. Making sure that a hacker can't forge the directives to open your house door or car doors. Oh, that happens. Not good when it does.

Availability refers to the ability to access information or resources when required. If someone is doing a Denial of Service on your house or your Internet provider, you can't get to your door lock. Yes, even with an Internet-connected door lock, you should take your physical key along. And don't set the access code to your birthday.

In this chapter, I am going to talk about some IOT applicable techniques for addressing all three parts of the Triad. The CIA Triad is shown in Figure 7-1.

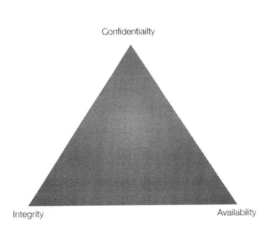

Figure 7-1. The CIA Triad

What Are the Dangers?

The dangers of computer insecurity depends on your information type and actuators of your IOT device. First, let's talk about information types.

The danger of hacking your device to gain information completely depends on the "value" of the information, both in a local sense and in a temporal sense. For example, a sensor reading the temperature in your closet probably isn't worth very much at any one time and knowing the temperature of your closet ten hours ago (temporal value) is probably even worth less.

Going the other direction, transmitting your password for your WiFi in the clear from an IOT device is a valuable piece of information; and in most systems, it is still valuable from ten hours in the past.

So, the value of information has two main components. Is the information valuable at the time of production, and does it continue to remain valuable as time advances?

Assigning Value to Information

In a real sense, the ultimate risk of data disclosure can be described as the value of the information disclosed. In the recent Target store information loss, it was expensive. The value of the information lost (credit card and customer information) was high, not only in fraud, but in fraud prevention (replacing all those cards) and eventually cost the CEO of Target his job. Now, note, because of these remedial actions, the time value of the information lost declined rapidly after the disclosure. What was the value of the information lost to Target? Somewhere around $10 or $15 million. While that might seem like a lot of money, it was less than 1 percent of the company's revenues.

After reimbursement from insurance and minus tax deductions, it was probably even less. The startling conclusion after looking at the reports is that big data breaches don't cost all that much to these companies. Similar numbers and costs apply to the Sony and the Home Depot data breaches. The costs just aren't material to these large companies.

All the consumers inconvenienced by getting new credit cards, or having fraud on their card, or their identity stolen would probably feel differently.

On a much smaller scale, I have experienced this on a more personal level. In 2000, I started a bank (yes, a real FDIC-insured actual bank) and have served on the board of directors since then. Naturally, I have served as chairman of the Technology Committee. It's been interesting.

In the mid-2000s, our Visa payment provider was compromised and we had a small fraud problem with the compromised cards (around $2,000) that the regulations say we were responsible for. We also had about $10,000 of cost in issuing new cards. We got a small reimbursement from our cyber-insurance but we had to go after the payment provider. After six months that went nowhere (they didn't want to pay anything even if it was clearly their fault), we gave up. So who really pays in this case? You, the consumer, with higher costs passed on to you.

Most academic papers focus on the cost of data loss and exposure in large- and medium-size enterprises. There is surprisingly little work about the cost of information loss and exposure in IOT.

So, how do you assign value to information in the IOT? You look at what it means to the user to have the data lost or compromised and estimate a financial (or personal) harm to the user. The companies above focus on cost to themselves. In the IOT you need to look at the cost to the end user.

What happens if someone hacks your front wireless door lock? How about your TV? According to reports, the Samsung Smart TV listens to you even when you aren't talking to the TV. They warn you not to discuss sensitive information around your TV. Good grief. When it was disclosed that it was possible to hack into the Samsung Smart TV camera on the top of the set, they suggested putting black tape over it or pushing it into the set with a pencil. Samsung is a $180 billion a year company. You would think they would put a little more into computer security.

Gartner forecasts [`www.gartner.com/newsroom/id/3165317`] that there will be 6.4 billion IOT "things" connected by the end of 2016. And they further forecast that by 2020 it will be 20 billion "things" connected. Using the rough numbers of the amount Gartner forecasts that will be spent on the global IOT security market (about $7 billion in 2015 and increasing to $30 billion in 2020), we come up with an interesting number. The amount that will be spent on securing the IOT will be about $1 per IOT device. Now this is something we can use in our budgeting for IOT development. My gut feel is that is about right.

Back to the value of information. In 2016, 5.5 million IOT devices get connected every day. These devices being connected include cars, kitchen appliances, smart TVs, wristwatches, toys, medical instruments, etc., etc.

When an IOT device gets connected, it needs to be protected.

Building The Three Basic Security Components for IOT Computers

Computer security is a complex topic with lots of interactions between different systems and subsystems in even a simple transaction from an IOT device to a server across the Internet. We are going to now return to the CIA Triad (Confidentiality, Integrity, and Availability) and see what we can do with each of these concepts in practice on these small computers.

Confidentiality - Cryptography

Confidentiality is defined as concealment of information. As was mentioned earlier, you can almost always get information out of device if you have physical access to the device. What we are focusing on in this section is protecting the information transmission channel rather than the physical IOT device itself.

Note from no. 2 above, obscurity doesn't count as far as computer security goes. If we are transmitting valuable information, then we need to encrypt it using cryptographic techniques. What is cryptography? Cryptographic techniques include uses for all of the CIA Triad, but here we are going to focus on encryption that is a subset of these techniques.

Discussing cryptography and encryption techniques can easily fill an entire book so I will stay away from the math and focus on the application. The one thing we do need to discuss is that modern cryptography is very heavily based on math and computer science methodologies. All of these techniques below can be broken based on the theoretical considerations of the algorithms, but it is impractical to do so by any known techniques. That makes these techniques "Computationally Secure." Someday in the future they may be able to read your thermometer, but will it be worth it? Depends on the value of the information.

There is one important thing to realize about encryption and cryptography. These algorithms tend to be computationally expensive in terms of amount of CPU clocks and RAM memory to do these calculations. Remember that IOT devices don't have a lot of CPU clocks or a lot of RAM memory. Therefore, use the minimum amount of these techniques to protect your data. You need to be smart to save battery and RAM space.

Cryptography on the Arduino

There are basically two ways for Arduino to communicate with external devices. You either have a network connection (Ethernet, Bluetooth, WiFi, Zigbee, or other networks), or you have a serial connector (USB, straight serial). While the techniques described in this section are applicable to both kinds of connections, we will focus on the network-type techniques. For the Arduino I am going to focus on using AES. While this next example is run on Arduino Mega2560, it can also be run on an ESP8266 with minimal changes.

AES is what they call a symmetric block cipher used by the U.S. government to protect classified information. It's pretty good encryption and can't be broken at the writing of this chapter by brute force attacks. However, as Bruce Shinier has said, "Attacks always get better; they never get worse."

Following are just some of the AES libraries available for the Arduino:

- `github.com/DavyLandman/AESLib`

- `spaniakos.github.io/AES/index.html`

- `utter.chaos.org.uk:/~markt/AES-library.zip`

We are using an Arduino Mega2560 (shown in Figure 7-2) instead of an Arduino Uno because the Mega2560 has 8K bytes of SRAM available versus 2K bytes in the Uno.

Figure 7-2. *Arduino Mega2560*

We are going to use the Davy Landman library for our examples. To install into your Arduino library, follow the directions in the README.md file. Following is an example of how to use the AES library in an Arduino program. You can substitute any Arduino for this example. However, it does not compile under the ESP8266 Arduino IDE unless changes are made to the AES library itself.

```
//
//
// AES Library Test
// SwitchDoc Labs
// February 2016
//

#include <AESLib.h>

// 256 bit key for AES
uint8_t key[] = {0, 1, 2, 3, 4, 5, 6, 7, 8, 9, 10, 11, 12, 13, 14, 15, 16,
17, 18, 19, 20, 21, 22, 23, 24, 25, 26, 27, 28, 29, 30, 31};
```

```
void setup() {

  Serial.begin(115200);
}

void loop() {
  // put your main code here, to run repeatedly:

  // 16 bytes
  char data[] = "01234567890Hello";

  int sizeOfArray;
  int i;

  sizeOfArray = sizeof(data) / sizeof(char);

  Serial.println();

  Serial.print("data to be encrypted (ASCII format):\t ");
  Serial.println(data);

  Serial.print("data to be encrypted (Hex format):\t ");

  for (i = 0;  i < sizeOfArray - 1; i++)
  {
    if (uint8_t(data[i]) < 0x10)
      Serial.print("0");
    Serial.print(uint8_t(data[i]), HEX);

  }
  Serial.println();

  // Now we encrypt the data using a 256 byte AES key

  aes256_enc_single(key, data);

  // print the encrypted data out in Hex

  Serial.print("encrypted (in Hex):\t\t\t ");

  for (i = 0; i < sizeOfArray - 1; i++)
  {
    if (uint8_t(data[i]) < 0x10)
      Serial.print("0");
    Serial.print(uint8_t(data[i]), HEX);

  }
  Serial.println();
```

```
// Now decrypt the data and print it out

aes256_dec_single(key, data);
Serial.print("decrypted:\t\t\t\t ");
Serial.println(data);
}
```

Note the key given at the beginning of the program. This 256-bit key is what you need both to encrypt and decrypt the data. Granted, this is not a very good key in our example.

Below is an example of the results of the program:

```
data to be encrypted (ASCII format):   01234567890Hello
data to be encrypted (Hex format):     303132333435363738393048656C6C6F
encrypted (in Hex):                    438693C632D91AF2283651F416BBA61E
decrypted:                             01234567890Hello
```

This is the single piece of secret information. Both ends of the communication channel need to have this key for AES to work.

Key management (how to send these keys around) is a key topic of IOT computer security design and will be discussed later in this chapter.

Looking at this program, you could see how you could decompile this code and retrieve the secret key. This is an example of why physical access to the device can often lead to the ability to hack the device and then the network of devices.

How fast are these libraries on an Arduino? Based on a 16MHz ATMega328, a 128-bit AES key can generate about 27,000 bytes per second. Using a 256-bit key gets you about 20,000 bytes per second.

Now that is full bore CPU usage, so if you have other things to do with the processor (as is almost certainly the case), you won't be able to make these data rates continuously.

Note that AES libraries are already built into the firmware for the ESP8266, but as of the writing of this chapter there really are no complete examples of how to use them and the documentation is very sparse.

Cryptography on the Raspberry Pi

The Raspberry Pi has a far richer set of cryptography libraries available in the operating system or as easily available downloads. For example, if you are communicating using web requests (between Raspberry Pi's or Linux-based computers), you can use SSL to encrypt the traffic between the two nodes. It is highly standardized, and if properly configured is strongly secure. Why don't we use SSL on an Arduino or ESP8266-based system? Two reasons: first, memory / processing power limitations; and second is the problem of distribution of the certificates necessary for secure SSL links. This is another variant of the key distribution problem.

The same AES-256 functions are available on the Raspberry Pi so they could be used in communicating with an Arduino. However, this method is a long way from the full SSL implementation used by modern web browsers and computer (think https:// instead of http://).

The Spaniakos AES encryption library as cited above under the Cryptography on the Arduino section is also available for the Raspberry Pi.

Note that there are hardware implementations of AES starting to appear for Arduinos and Raspberry Pi.

Integrity - Authentication

Integrity is defined as the trustworthiness of the data or resources. Note the difference between Integrity and Encryption. When I speak of integrity, I am speaking of making sure that the directives or data sent to my IOT device has not been changed en route and that I know for sure who sent it. The directives or data may or may not be encrypted.

Looking at this from a value-of-information perspective, this means that we don't really care if a hacker looks at the data (I am turning up the heat in my house), but we use integrity to make sure that a hacker cannot forge the directive or data and that the hacker cannot change the data itself.

There are many ways of using cryptographic algorithms for establishing the integrity of the contents of the message and establishing who sent the message.

Establishing that the message has not been changed en route can be done by using what is called a cryptographic hash on the message. In concept, you take each byte of the message and by using a cryptographic algorithm, you can determine that the message has not been changed – with a very, very high degree of certainty.

Cryptographic Hashes on the Arduino / Raspberry Pi

In order to prove that the message has not been altered on transit, you will need to send the message + the hash across the network. Much like the encryption example above, you need to take your message and cryptographically hash the message to generate the hash codes. We will use the fork from Cathedrow library [https://github.com/maniacbug/Cryptosuite] for this example.

However, the libraries required some tweaking to make them work in the newer versions of the Arduino IDE, so I have included them in the download of this software as additional tabs. This will work with an Arduino board and an ESP8266 board.

```
//
// SHA256 Hash Test
//
// For both the Arduino and ESP8266
// SwitchDoc Labs
//
// February 2016

#include "sha256.h"
```

```
void printHash(uint8_t* hash) {
  int i;
  for (i = 0; i < 32; i++) {
    Serial.print("0123456789abcdef"[hash[i] >> 4]);
    Serial.print("0123456789abcdef"[hash[i] & 0xf]);
  }
  Serial.println();
}

void setup() {

  Serial.begin(115200);
  Serial.println("SHA256 Hash Test");
    Serial.println();

}

void loop() {

  uint8_t *hash;
  Sha256.init();
  String hashMessage;
  int i;

  while (1)
  {

    hashMessage = "This is a message to hash-";
    hashMessage = hashMessage + String(i % 10);
    Serial.print("Hashing Message: ");
    Serial.println(hashMessage);
    Sha256.print(hashMessage);

    hash = Sha256.result();

    printHash(hash);
    Serial.println();
    delay(5000);

    i++;

  }

}
```

The results are as follows:

```
SHA256 Hash Test
Hashing Message: This is a message to hash-2
f2a47cefff87600aeb9089cf1f11a51b833ccdd91b808df75b7238fc78ba53f2

Hashing Message: This is a message to hash-3
5d135bc35a33004cad4c4ed37fc0011c1475f09c6ddd7dec01c348734e575f41

Hashing Message: This is a message to hash-4
fe1aa898ab0e041d1ce4539b388439c75a221efab0672896fc5e14b699c01492
```

If the hashed message is changed, the SHA256 hash will change. You can say that the message has not been changed en route to your device. Note we have no cryptographic key to exchange. SHA256 will work the same everywhere.

SwitchDoc Note   Proving something has not been altered in transit will tell you it is good. However, what if we just have a slightly corrupted message? This could be caused by noise in the line (think satellite communication). If you want to correct errors in a message like this, a whole other set of algorithms is used. Reed-Solomon error correction codes are a great example of these. You can correct the data, then decrypt it. Obviously, you need to encrypt the message first and then put these codes over the top of the encrypted data to make your communication channel more reliable. Reversing the order (encrypting the Reed-Solomon code) makes no sense and will not provide error correction.

The Raspberry Pi code is very similar.

So, this seems pretty straightforward. What are we missing? We have the proof that the message has not been changed. Great. Proof of data integrity.

However, we have not proved that the data has not been forged using a man-in-the-middle attack. Now we have to look at the last part of data integrity. Proof where it is coming from, or in other words, non-repudiation.

Non-repudiation is usually based upon some variation of Public/Private Key Encryption.

It works like this. Bob has a private key, only known to him. He also has a public key that he gives to anybody who wants to communicate with him. When Bob wants to send a message to Alice, he encodes the message with his private key and sends it to Alice. Alice uses the public key she got from Bob to decrypt the message. If it successfully decrypts, then Alice knows that the message came from Bob.

So, using this public/private key method, we can encrypt the message and prove it came from Bob and is unaltered. Reversing the procedure, we can send a message to Bob from Alice safely.

OK, looks perfect. What are the complications? Once again we are back to key exchanges. Both our IOT server and the IOT device have to have private keys and publish public keys to the server. This does sound like a lot of work. And it is. Those more-sophisticated readers will notice that this sounds a lot like SSH/HTTPS. Correct. And as noted above, those are big libraries for small computers, although the Raspberry Pi can handle it, the Arduino class of processors really can't. The ESP8266 is barely able to do this (and does it for their over the air update option) but they are not distributing keys. They update a one-way communication. For bidirectional communication links, you need keys for both directions.

There is a whole additional level of complexity laid on top of this. Certificates must be traceable to a known trusted authority to prove the system hasn't been compromised.

Showing examples of the public/private key software is well beyond the scope of this book. Some keywords to look for are "Digital Signature, Diffie-Hellman, and RSA Public Key Encryption" when searching for this technology. A good example of a system showing this kind of a system between an Arduino and a Windows PC is available at this link: github.com/arpitchauhan/cryptographic-protocols-arduino-and-PC/

The overall methodology used is as follows:

- Public keys are exchanged securely between the two devices (note: both have their own private key).

- After the Public keys are exchanged, you can transfer a key for AES encryption.

- Now the devices can communicate securely and safely using AES as in the example above.

An important thing to remember is public/private key encryption is much more computationally expensive than AES encryption. This is why you exchange your AES keys with this scheme and then just use AES to send the data in normal operation.

Availability - Handling DOS / Loss of Server / Watchdogs

There really isn't a lot of difference between an attack to deny you service (DOS), the Internet going down, your wireless router rebooting, or your microwave oven going crazy. All of these things disrupt your communication path to your IOT device.

One thing that commercial wireless IOT devices are especially vulnerable to is the inability to talk to the server because of electrical noise in the environment whether generated by error or on purpose. When you are planning your IOT device, you need to make sure you design it so your device can handle a disruption of communication service, whether it is done on purpose or by equipment failure. There needs to be some method for telling the user or consumer that you have a fault.

How does the military get around this? It uses complex schemes like frequency hopping radios, large amounts of radiated radio power to "burn through" the noise, and big antennas. These are not techniques that are cheaply available to our IOT devices.

Key Management

Key management is a hard problem. Configuration management of IOT devices is difficult. From the sections earlier in this chapter, we need to have a shared key to do AES256 encryption to keep our communication confidential. We also need keys to prove that the message has come from the correct person or server.

Remember that ANY time your IOT device is communicating with the Internet or the local area network, there is a possibility of compromise.

There are two approaches to key management on IOT devices. The first is by using hardware key management.

Companies like Infineon build chips that include private and public keys that can be used to build networks of IOT devices. You can establish trusted certificates (linking to a trusted certificate authority) at the time of manufacture and then establishing a set of software protocols for using these keys after deployment. As the process and chips become less expensive, I believe we will see more and more of these types of systems deployed. At the writing of this book, these chips are not cheap. Using one will roughly double the price of your IOT device in many cases. What about physical access to these devices? Yes, you can compromise a device by taking it and tearing it apart (and I don't just mean taking the screws out. I'm talking about removing the plastic from the chips and going through the chip with a microscope. Remember our discussion about the value of information? It's probably not worth doing all of this to compromise your thermostat or toaster.

The second method is to use software to distribute the keys during configuration (or even during manufacturing). These methods in general are called PKI (Public Key Infrastructure).

Generally, many IOT devices are more vulnerable to attacks than normal servers, PCs, and smartphones because they operate with embedded software (firmware) that has been developed without online security in mind. There are many examples of really bad software flaws that can include back-end management with default passwords that are easily found on the Internet and non-encrypted communications. People are actively hacking into things like routers and other connected devices and using them in DOS (Denial Of Service) attacks. Think of our LightSwarm devices in a previous chapter. You could program them all to start sending messages as quickly as possible and create your own DOS attack. During the development of the LightSwarm, I inadvertently did that very thing. I overwhelmed the Raspberry Pi server by sending messages all at once, as quickly as possible.

Another real issue with IOT devices is that the internal IOT device firmware may not be updated for years (or the company may go out of business) and the infrastructure for updating these devices just doesn't exist or not.

The use of current PKI methods are just impractical to scale to the upcoming multiple billions of IOT devices projected to be connected to the network. Because of this many manufacturers take short cuts to secure their devices. For example, all of the IOT devices may share a single key (either an AES encryption key or a single public/private key pair). This method does supply a significant amount of security, but if the single key is compromised (as has happened many times in the computer industry. Think Sony and Microsoft) then the entire network is open to hackers.

The industry has the mathematic and technical tools to protect the IOT. What we don't have is a simple and secure method for distributing the keys to all of the IOT.

This is a problem that has not been solved yet and probably won't be before we deploy another few billion computers.

Update Management

According to one pundit (actually me), the two biggest problems for keeping IOT devices safe are the following:

- Lack of remote updating capability
- Remote updating capability

Being able to update your firmware is key to avoiding obsolescence and to recover from flaws that come to light after deployment of devices. This is one very important channel of information that needs to be cryptographically secured, both from a data integrity point of view and to make sure it is only being updated from where it should be updated from (non-repudiation). The techniques above can be used to do these very things.

If anybody can figure out how to fool your updating system, the person can reprogram your entire system.

Conclusion

Why would someone want to break into your thermostat? To provide an entrance to your network. Remember the Target data breach I talked about earlier? That was initiated via a cooling system maintenance application. They got in the network via the air conditioner.

The IOT represents a huge opportunity to improve people's lives and experiences. With great power comes great responsibility. When you design your Internet Of Things killer application and device, design security in from the beginning. Don't tack it on at the end.

Watch the news. In the near future, you will see articles about people (and programs) hacking into cars – oh wait, they are already doing that. You will see articles about people hacking into hotel door locks – oh wait, they are already doing that. And you will see people hacking into your home thermostat – oh wait, they are already doing that, too.

Following is an example from an Amazon review:

> The man wrote that his wife had left him for another man and then moved her new man into their old home that they had shared, which had a Honeywell WiFi thermostat. The ex-lover could still control the thermostat through the mobile app installed on his smartphone, so he used it to change the environment for the couple now living in his old house:

> "Since this past Ohio winter has been so cold I've been messing with the temp while the new lovebirds are sleeping. Doesn't everyone want to wake up at 7 a.m. to a 40 degree house? When they are away on their weekend getaways, I

crank the heat up to 80 degrees and back down to 40 before they arrive home. I can only imagine what their electricity bills might be. It makes me smile. I know this won't last forever, but I can't help but smile every time I log in and see that it still works. I also can't wait for warmer weather when I can crank the heat up to 80 degrees while the lovebirds are sleeping. After all, who doesn't want to wake up to an 80 degree home in the middle of June?"

Now granted, that isn't really a technical hack – more of a social engineering experience, but it shows what can be done with these little systems.

Your Nest Thermostat (insert your own IOT example here) can be a gateway into your home. In many systems, like the Nest Thermostat, you are only one password from being hacked. Makes a good argument for good passwords on ANY system that is exposed to the Internet.

And remember that all devices are vulnerable to being hacked with physical access. So make sure you keep your "real" metal keys safe, too.

APPENDIX

▩ ▩ ▩

Suggestions for Further Work

The IOT is an area of active research and now active deployment. Nobody in the industry has yet found the "killer application" that will take the IOT to mass consumer deployment, but it is just a matter of time. If you took the time to build the IOT projects in the previous chapters, you now have a basic set of skills to prototype and innovate in the IOT space. There is no better way of learning a new set of abilities than actually building things. That is the mantra of the Maker Movement.

Following are some of the IOT projects that I am currently working on. They are good suggestions for further work on your own, if you are so inclined.

- OurWeather - a no-soldering required IOT Weather Station kit for ages 8 and up

- Air Quality IOT device

- Low Power RF Links for IOT devices

- SunRover - Solar Powered IOT Connector Robot

- SunGrassHopper - IOT Connected small solar-powered robot

- Cloud Cover Detecting IOT sensor

- Building IOT Devices using Grove Connectors for easy and fast prototyping

Another idea is to regularly scour the following web sites for new devices and new sensors:

- www.sparkfun.com

- www.adafruit.com

- www.seeedstudio.com

- www.tinysine.com

For more technical users:

- www.digkey.com

- www.mouser.com

- www.texasinstruments.com

© John C. Shovic 2016
J. C. Shovic, *Raspberry Pi IoT Projects*, DOI 10.1007/978-1-4842-1377-3

When I see a new sensor that is interesting, I jump on it, build a project, and publish it in either magazines or on my blog. There are new IOT base devices (like the Adafruit Huzzah) coming online every day. If you see one and you are interested, buy it and build something. Come visit my blog and join the conversation at www.switchdoc.com.

Parting Words . . .

The IOT is going to be big. Just how big, nobody knows. The technologies that are now exploding in the marketplace are accessible to the reasonably technically minded person. As always, I feel the best learning is by the doing. If you have built the five projects in this book, then you have a really good idea of what is going on with the devices in your household or workplace. IOT probably doesn't mean "Black Box" to the reader anymore.

Have you ever heard of Metcalfe's Law? It states that "the value of a telecommunications network is proportional to the square of the number of connected users of the system."

Substitute "connected IOT Device" for "connected users" and read it again. The world is at the cusp of something. It might just be bigger than the Internet. Oh wait. It will be the Internet. The Internet Of Things will be much larger than the Internet of connected people.

Keep reading the blogs and building things. Stay current with the technology and the future won't be nearly as mysterious as it was when you started this book.

Index

© John Shovic 2016
J. Shovic, *Raspberry Pi IoT Projects*, DOI 10.1007/978-1-4842-1377-3

Get the eBook for only $5!

Why limit yourself?

Now you can take the weightless companion with you wherever you go and access your content on your PC, phone, tablet, or reader.

Since you've purchased this print book, we're happy to offer you the eBook in all 3 formats for just $5.

Convenient and fully searchable, the PDF version enables you to easily find and copy code—or perform examples by quickly toggling between instructions and applications. The MOBI format is ideal for your Kindle, while the ePUB can be utilized on a variety of mobile devices.

To learn more, go to www.apress.com/companion or contact support@apress.com.

74529330R00146

Made in the USA
San Bernardino, CA
17 April 2018